Distant Corners in a Crowded Room

by Om Prakash

Distant Corners in a Crowded Room
All Rights Reserved © January 21, 2007

ISBN: 978-0-615-25504-0

John W. Gilmore, D. Min.
Friends of Sat Yoga Costa Rica
Philadelphia, PA 19144
www.dswellness.com
©January 2008

Acknowledgments

The ideas and concepts collected in this books come from many inspirational sources. It is not my intention to create yet another text- book, or yet another book on spirituality. This book is an overview of life, how it works, and how we can be free from the binding effects of the underlying matrix of thoughts, ideas, and energies that comprise the ego and cause us to lose contact with our, true, divine selves and become trapped in Maya (the illusion we call reality).

The sources of inspiration are the precepts of Creation Spirituality, as purported by Dr., Rev. Matthew Fox, founder of the University of Creation Spirituality; the ongoing exploration of Dr., Rev. Om Prakash John Gilmore, Director of Friends of Sat Yoga Costa Rica (pertaining to understanding identity based oppression, overcoming it and healing from its effects), and lastly, the teachings of Shunyamurti Robert Shubow, PhD., founder of Sat Yoga Institute in Costa Rica. The teachings from Sat Yoga are the underlying foundation that pulls together all of the other thoughts and philosophies presented here into one powerful explanation of how the world works. For that reason we have emboldened all of the teachings from Sat Yoga Institute so they may be recognized as part of the Sat Yoga Philosophy.

Previous Books

Reunion of Souls

The Keran Chronicles I, II, and III

The Keran Chronicles I: Kera King and Queen

The Keran Chronicles II: The Phases of Kera

The Keran Chronicles III: Into the Darkness of Kera

Life, Work, and Spirituality

Reclaiming the Religion of Jesus in a Modern Age

The Keran Chronicles IV: Fulfilling the Prophecies

Distant Corners in a Crowded Room

by Om Prakash

The window opened for a brief moment. I saw a blue, shinning sky woven together with clouds and golden sunshine. Captured within its matrix...a beautiful thing, a golden presence more beautiful than the blueness of the sky. This beauty was the foundation of nature— the beauty that was the essence of nature; it was beauty, it was life, it was love in every sense of the word. And then, just like a curtain being drawn or a door being slammed, it was gone. There I was alone again on a barren planet trying to create light out of darkness, beauty out of cruelty, and love out of fear.

Om Prakash John W. Gilmore

To Obtain Power
Section 1

Being Self-Sufficient
Chapter 1

Life can be a challenge for most of us. We are born through the pain of our mothers. We share in that pain, as we are squeezed out through an opening a bit too small into glaring lights, a lot of unfamiliar noise, and a room full of motion and strange surroundings. Sometimes we are even cut out. In many instances we are struck on the back-side to introduce us to our first breath. The blow and the pain that goes with it is our first experience of feeling in the physical body. The feeling is so devastating to us that it makes us cry out and take our first breath. When we think of a child being struck and taking its first breath we think of it joyfully because a new life has just entered into the world. The baby cries and the parents are elated. It has come into the world and is alive and fully functioning.

When we think of this occurrence from the child's point of view, however, from the deep recesses of our subconscious where we have experienced the shock, it is horrible and devastating.

"Labour and birth are a relatively short time period relatively speaking, but it is the monumental task of leaving a symbiotic state with the mother and becoming, within seconds, a physiologically independent being. How this done does matter -- "under the influence," afraid, stressed, defensive, etc., or peaceful, lovingly, gently, safely does matter. What mother feels baby experiences -- and it is apart of the early brain. It is known that the LIMBIC system of the brain -- that stores emotion --is on-line in the last trimester through first year of life. No other time is as critical in establishing very important neural programming.[1]"

In truth this experience is so devastating that we begin to lose our true identities when all of this occurs. In truth we are divine beings. We are the essence of the universe, shoved down and corked into a body that we call the human form. When we entered the body as new born babies it was unruly; it couldn't walk; it couldn't talk--left alone the body would have been devoured by the elements of time, or by organisms that lurk everywhere out of eyesight waiting to fill themselves with the tender flesh of this new body and to send our essences pouring out--back out into the universe that we have so easily forgotten.

We are born anew. With our limited minds in this body we struggle to make sense of the new sights, sounds, and experiences. For the first time we feel fear, vulnerability, love, and uncertainty. We are divine souls. In a last ditched effort to save ourselves we use the last bit of our god-like

creative energy that we have before we forget who we are to divide off a part of ourselves to serve as a system or institution within our heads to preserve us. This part of our mind will sustain us and keep us whole. It will record our experiences and provide us with life's tools. It will support us through the dark times until we can be self sufficient, like the beings we were before we came to this plane. Our last effort is successful. We have created something to help us, guide us, and protected us. We have created the ego.[2] With the ego in place we simply forget who we really are and what we have **always been,** we become servants of the institution consisting of the ego, the censor, the conscious, and the subconscious.

Living in the fog is easy and exciting for several years as we learn to take bowel movements, as we learn to eat, to move, and to walk. We are actually mastering the bodies in which we find ourselves and realizing that our words, cries, and bodies can manipulate the world around us. We can create things. We can change things. Tears and anger at the right time can make our caregivers, friends, and family surrender and bend to our wills and do our biding.

We can also become servants and bend to the wills of others who have the power to reward us as we mimic their actions and beliefs. If we can repeat things back the way they want them, we are rewarded. They make us feel good inside, and special. The only problem is that it gets harder and harder to feel special. When we begin to feel special our censor takes over. It cuts off the thoughts and

10

feelings that make us feel special so that it can return us to the time when it and the ego were first created. The censor loves sameness and stability so it takes us back to the way we were feeling before we felt special. We begin to need more and more attention to feel special, because there is never enough. The censor is always removing the special feeling in order to return us to the initial creation of it and the ego. Our life begins to become a life of just seeking nurturance and warmth.

We learn words, we write down letters which are symbols for words, we add numbers and if we do it right, the big man or woman at the front of the classroom who seems to have all of the power really make us feel good. They put stars on our papers and an "A" for excellence. They pin them up to a board or door for everyone to see. Every time someone looks at that paper and sees our name along with that star they know that we are excellent. If we get more papers pinned to the board for every subject, we get privileges. We make the adults smile. Our parents brag about us more and laugh more, telling their friends how great we are. We have succeeded. Our last creation as a divine being worked. We are getting control of our lives in this new world. If we are not getting golden stars, there is a problem.

When we get a "B" sometimes the smiling faces say, "Oh, you only got five wrong. You can do better next time." "Cs" and "D" turn the smile upside down into frowns. "Fs" turn the smiles into anger, the shaking of the

head or the clucking of the tongue. Too many "Fs" create jeering, laughter and mockery; we are told that we are stupid, lazy and worthless.—destined to be at the bottom and to live on the street. We are being shaped and manipulated, but we can't feel it. All we can feel is the disappointment projected onto us, or the joy. Our life begins to consist of seeking one and rejecting the other.[3]

The one with the "A" fights to maintain the "As" and to be successful in all of her endeavors to keep receiving endorsement that says she is better. The one who gets the "Fs" finds a different path. It can be sports, it can be violence, and it can be studying hard to overcome her deficiencies. Whatever he chooses becomes a pattern that sets him on a course for the rest of his life. This pattern will affect the attitudes, and behaviors he will carry the rest of his life and that will carry him. This pattern of thoughts and behaviors will blossom into his life story. If there is no great change in the script, he will live and die according to this narrative without even being aware. His loved ones won't tell him, because they too are living by internalized narratives and various circumstances their lives have created.

Every decision and choice of behaviors and attitudes that help to relieve immediate pain will increase the possibility of the same behavioral choice occurring more often. The more often it occurs, the more often her mental system, her ego, will repeat it and strengthen the possibility of it occurring. The ego will become stronger and stronger with every successful choice until it is seen as superior and dominant. Eventually the real *she* will become like a baby tree growing in a flower pot. She won't be able to spread her leaves or her roots. She may be beautiful or powerful in a limited sort of way, but will never be able to reach her full potential in such a little pot. **She will begin to think that her given name, the thoughts and beliefs given to her and the part that she has created is her true self, and that any other image, or the true, divine self that is really her is just a mirage.**[4]

Facing the Dilemma
Chapter 2

We are making it through life successfully. We are getting stroked and rewarded, or kicked and beaten, but at least we know what to expect. Through kindness, love, anger, or violence we can even manipulate the world ourselves in order to meet our immediate needs. But to get more, we need to plan more. We need to plot more and strengthen our egos to get more pleasure and less pain. There doesn't seem to be a way to do that unless we choose the best path—the best course of action in the world. The best course seems to be the one that most people agree upon. Trying to figure out what people agree upon from one moment to the other will take a lot of time and energy, so we must devise a way to do it automatically. We do this through the ego that we have created. As time goes on our ego takes on more

responsibilities and becomes more fractured, diverse, and powerful. It needs to maintain its level of energy. To do so it constantly reconfigures itself.

Through the prompting of the ego we learn to choose the thoughts, feelings, and attitudes that create the behaviors that we want the most and make them automatic. How can we do this? We can begin to take in the information that strengthens our egos and discard what does not. We can create another part called the personality. This personality can include actions and reactions, thoughts and behaviors that occur in a pattern so we really don't have to think about it. If we can do this and can create a competent workable personality, we can enhance the pleasure and joy that we need to diminish the pain that can occur in the world, and the pain that is stored in the subconscious as images and fantasies of our fears and unfulfilled desires..

We can only do this by blocking out all that doesn't fit into this personality, or set of beliefs. We can shove the characteristics that don't find down into our subconscious to never be seen again, and use a little of our energy to keep them down. We can form a *censor* out of all of the rules that we hear and the rewards or punishments for actions that we see. The censor will be like an Executive Board in the ego, as if the ego is an institution. The censor is will be a part of the mind that helps keep those thoughts that just don't fit deep in the unconscious, and it can also steer the incoming thoughts that don't fit away from the conscious and the ego, and drive them down into the subconscious. It can guarantee us a more stable life. We can freeze our world and keep it as it is.

The censor begins as a servant just as the institution begins as a servant to a community or a society. It works very well on automatic. The problem is that things that work automatically usually cannot be stopped, or corrected. What ultimately happens, therefore, is that the censor, like the ego, becomes a prisoner that we must eventually break through to be free, and to reclaim our true identities as divine beings, according to Shunyamurti Robert Shubow, founder of Sat Yoga Institute. With the help of this invisible, automatic censor we can freeze time, or at least slow it down to a speed where we feel comfortable in our limited bodies. The creation of the illusion of frozen time is valuable because it allows us to create things on the material plane. We can feel love, peace and harmony on this earth as we mature and become the creators that we were as divine beings. The problem is that we forget that we are the one's creating the illusion. We begin to live the illusion as if it were real, instead of an instrument to enhance our well being.

While we are working hard to create a personality, we are creating a *shadow personality*. It is the opposite of the one that we show to everyone. It is invisible, but it is always there. A lot of energy is being used to hold it down.[5] We could be using that energy to create life, or enjoy our relationships, instead it is used to press down the parts of ourselves that we don't accept. With the complexities of life

and all of the energy that we must expend in daily living we slip sometimes and those unacceptable parts emerge every so often. The older we get and the weaker we become and the stronger they become so that it takes much more effort and energy to shove them down, but we have to hold them down; we have forgotten our true identities so we have no choice. We fear that we will go insane if they are allowed to pop up all over the place. We see them as the other. We think of them as sick, alien thoughts entering in into our heads, which is a sure sign of mental illness. That is what the world tells us, anyway.

We cannot remember our divine selves and reconnect with the creative divine energy in the world, the divine part of ourselves known as Atman, so we have to find our creativity somewhere else. As we break free from the first relationship that we have, that which takes place with our primary caregiver, we are left alone. This relationship, and the images projected onto us are the only nurturance that we know as beings, even if they are brutal and painful. We are always seeking someone who will replace her and give us the same type of love and nurturance we received then, or we will fight against that type of treatment by seeking someone who is different in many aspects. If we cannot find that type of person while we are striving to be masters over this material world, we will live lives of emptiness and misery even if we are successful and our lives seem full to others.

"We want to find the essence of life," as Shubow says, "But all that we find is emptiness." **When we don't find the essence inside, we seek to find it outside of ourselves. We can get some of it from friends, some from our family, some from teachers, some from doing dangerous things and getting pumped full of adrenaline, or even from religion.**

The only way to really attain essence, however, is to go to the source of all essence. We can go directly to God, the source of all, to receive all that we want, but we will have to allow ourselves to change if we do that. We have already set up this personality and our life story; it is hard to dismantle. It is all hard to dismantle the ego, the censor, and the life story. If we find a group with something to offer and we cannot change our belief system to fit the groups how will we acquire the essence? How can we become part of the group? We can pretend. We can press down our real belief systems and act as though we are in total agreement. If we are not good enough at pretending we can lie to ourselves so much that we won't realize that we are pretending anymore, and then we will think we can get the power, the essence, that we need.

There is only one problem with doing this. If we lie enough to ourselves we will be swept away. We will change and the censor will change so that our lies will become real for us. We will be trapped in a bigger illusion that narrows our thinking and our choices in life ever more. Looking for freedom will have led us into a smaller cage. Eventually, having received the essence of the group, or the

life giving power of the group and their false beliefs, we will find that they

are not fulfilling in the long run. We will find that the essence that we have been seeking outside of ourselves is just emptiness in disguise, and then we will have to settle for a life of slow, painful death, or begin to seek again.

This can lead to a life where we settle for what we have. We lose all hope and live as people who don't reach high anymore and accept what we are given. We go to work, come home, watch television, and have a couple of beers. We do what we are supposed to do according to society without question. When we feel empty we fill our emptiness with sex, drugs, music, and even through identifying with the successes of our children sometimes. We think that we are free and we have everything, but there is often a nagging emptiness when we are alone with nothing present to fill up the emptiness. This is a life that Sat Yoga refers to as living in *The Zombie Box*. We can live trapped in that box going on automatic all of our lives, or we can be bold enough to break free. First, however, there is a tendency follow several paths as we continue to seek essence. We will discuss them in the following chapters.

To Obtain Satisfaction
Section 2

The Path of Family
Chapter 3

One path that we can take while seeking the essence is the path of developing close relationships with the family. We can find ways to please our mother, father, brothers and sisters. When the mother, or the primary care-giver cares for us and feeds us as children we form a bond with her. In our infant minds there is no separation between us and the mother. As we grow older, however, we find that she is not always there. We find that our cries for food and nurturance are not met as quickly as we would like, or someone else, some strange being, is coming to meet our needs.

As we grow older we see how Mother is giving some of her time and attention to the other...to a strange being. She is giving her attention to the Father, or a partner. We don't know what has happened. As a result of this...this disappearance of the nurturer, the disappearance of the breast, we find emptiness deep inside. It is as if part of us has been torn away and we are left empty. We are no longer whole. As we look to the care-giver's partner we can see that the partner has some type of power that we don't have. We begin to bond with the partner as we identify with him. We realize that he has a certain type of power. He has something that draws Mother away.

We realize that we can get this power by imitating him, or drawing close to him. We begin to take on his mannerisms and behaviors so we will be liked by the care-giver also. We are now involved in a triad instead of a dyad for the first time. **If it is a female child she will begin to seek someone like her father, unconsciously, because of the power he has over the mother. If it is a male child in a patriarchal society he will by to be like the father and gain power so he will have a female partner some day like the mother. In this way the society will be perpetuated. Women will look for powerful men and men will have to prove themselves powerful to get women. This, of course, is now changing as the society is less patriarchal, care-givers can now either be male or female, and women have more opportunities to obtain high-powered jobs.**

All of this identification, none-the-less, is a way to deal with the emptiness that a child has when she or he is separated from the mother (primary caregiver). It is as if we can actually draw the power from others by identifying with them. As long as we do that the emptiness seems to disappear. If we can get close to the parent, or get close to stronger brothers and sisters we can identify with them and be satisfied. We can compete with them and work hard to please our parents and find favor. Those of us who have separated from the breast in a healthy way can cover up the pain and suffering by refusing to recognize the emptiness--the hole that is deep inside our soul. We can fill it up by grabbing power. We can please people. We can gain self esteem by getting the "As," and by striving to be best. If we do we will feel superior, seeing ourselves as great people and eventually great leaders with much power. We can go on like this forever, but there is a hole inside that threatens to suck us in when we are alone. When we are away from all of the people and the bright lights we feel a horrible, sick, and depressed. It is a sickness of the soul that we may try to fill with drugs, money, excitement, sex, sexual perversion, but that doesn't work. Nothing works.

We please our family, but they begin to die. When siblings begin to form their own families and marry partners, or when they begin to work on their own careers they are too busy to deal with us. If we only depend on the family to fill our hole we will become disappointed, because they will not always be there. We will become someone who needs to "get a life" and move on. Placing all emphasis on family doesn't work.

If we start our own family the same things will eventually happen. Our partners and our children will feel smothered some day and will want to move on, and will want us to move on. The emptiness will come again after that, except with much more force. No matter what, we will have to deal with the emptiness. Shunyamurti describes this type of person in the Zombie Box as a *number one*. They want to be number one not realizing that number one is also the loneliest number. They don't admit to their loneliness, but it is always there guiding them and prodding them to go forward to outrun it. They become a slave to an invisible hunger and their censor freezes them in that phase, never allowing them to break free.

The only thing worse than being a one, is being a zero. Many ones were being produced when the patriarchal society was in full force. The child would see the father and understand that the father had all of the power—as in strength and material goods. The child would identify with the father and seek that power in order to gain mastery over the mother. Male children would seek the power of the father by working outside of themselves in order to gain material goods and machismo. Female children would seek to find someone like the father and imitate the behaviors of the mother to do so. There were, however, variances depending on the households and whether the children were gay or straight, or the parents. In earlier days, however, people were not so open about such issues.

Nowadays, with women working out of the household and exerting more power things are changing. The child often doesn't know with whom to identify. The child is left on its own, so to speak, to find a path. Sometimes, because of the confusion and no clear target, and if the separation between the caregiver (I will use the term mother referring to caregiver) is taken away or pulled away violently, the child never comes to term with it and is left with a gaping psychological wound.

The child becomes angry and has a sense of worthlessness. The child feels that he has been cheated and that he deserved better from his parents and life in general. He seeks essence from somewhere else, except angrily and violently. He hates the world and hates life. He climbs the ladder to gain power-over people and things, but he feels worthless. Sometimes he feels so distraught and worthless that he cannot gain any power and lives a life of desperation and emptiness. He cannot find any meaning and his life becomes a living hell as he realizes that he is empty and a zero. The difference between a one and a zero is that the zero knows that he or she is empty. The one deceives herself into thinking that she is full when she is really empty. Both types of people work constantly to find the essence out of life through many venues. If they cannot through family they extend their search to friends as their social circle widens.

The Path of Friends
Chapter 4

Those who are hungry for essence, or life energy, usually reach outside of their family to find it if it is not readily available through the family. Sometimes the influences from the family can seem oppressive; thoughts, rules, and requirements packed into the minds of a child can seem like hell on earth. The ego, looking for the best way to proceed through life often adopts those beliefs. When the child begins to please the parent in order to get what it needs it becomes a habit. The way that he or she pleases is recorded in part of the ego that is set aside as the super ego. All of the rules that teach us to please and to be good individuals, or to

24

at least be like our parents and the power people in society, will be a part of us forever. They are expressed by an internal voice that is often authoritarian and cynical telling us what we should do. Or evaluating our behaviors positively or negatively. This voice is overbearing sometimes.

The are only two ways to counteract this voice most of the time: One can do whatever the voice says and become a slave to the will of others projected as one's own thoughts, or one can fight like crazy to ignore it. This ignoring can either be rejecting it and doing the opposite of whatever it says, or being beaten down by it because and left in a state of depression because it cannot be quieted as we fail to meet its high standards. One way to bypass this whole process, especially for ones and zeros, is to find a set of friends who counteract the authoritarian voices.

During formative years, especially as a teenager, one can find friends who in no way resemble one's family, one's friend, or one's own culture. One finds people who are counter-cultural. They create their won thoughts, behaviors, and habits that go contrary to what the society holds dear. When the ones and the zeros meet they become a perfect match. The zero who knows he or she is empty gets nurturing from the powerful one who thinks that he or she is not empty. The one is full of the illusion of power not recognizing the hole at the center of herself while the zero draws on that power and is able to manipulate the one, because the zero can see the emptiness in the one and can use the illusion of fullness to move the one in whatever direction he or she would like by creating discomfort for the one. **When the one feels the discomfort of the emptiness being forced to the conscience, he or she will do whatever is necessary, power wise, the keep it submerged.**

The zero becomes a master at manipulating the one. The zero also has little respect for the one because the zero feels that he or she can see reality. He or she knows that the world is rotten and miserable, and that he or she is nothing. The one is delusional, because he or she thinks that they are something. What makes one something or nothing is how he or she deals with emptiness. In a group of counter-cultural peers one deals with emptiness in two ways: One maintains the illusion of power by rejecting everything that the society holds dear; and one maintains control over the less savvy by creating a culture that is even more stringent than any that the society could possibly maintain while pretending that there is none.

This can be seen in friendships where the good, *clean-cut* teenager who is dissatisfied with his life hangs around with a scruffy child with juvenile tendencies. The clean-cut kid has everything going for him and is a misfit in his society. Due to his status, however, he feels that he is a one and that he will help the juvenile become more. The juvenile knows that the clean-cut kid is an idiot and that the world is horrible. He keeps the clean-cut kid on a string and borrows money from him often, or gets him to do dangerous things like steal, or fight, to prove that he is a one.

During this friendship the zero is manipulating the one and gaining power over him, all of his education, and all of his money, through manipulation, thus raising his own self-esteem. The one who thinks he is superior actually thinks that he is helping the zero all along the way not realizing that he is being used and manipulated. All of this is taking place on a subconscious level, so both individuals may actually not even know they are doing this dance.

This is also something that used to take place between men and women. The man was supposed to have all of the power and make all of the money decisions. He had to seem strong to everyone, so once he made the decision he had to stand firm, especially if his wife insisted on getting something expensive.

Over time they develop a relationship where she begins to manipulate him to get what she wants. He pretends to be manipulated and gives her what she wants. He really wanted to give her what she wanted in the first place, but he would have appeared weak. They continually play this game as they dehumanize each other. He thinks that he is a one. She knows that she is a zero and that he is one too who thinks that he isn't. Out of lack of respect for him and his foolishness she manipulates him proving to herself that he is not a one at all. This is not as usual today as previously in the west, since many women can work for themselves in order to attain what they

27

need, but it was very normal behavior less than fifty years ago in the United States and in most of the western world. Both of these people are working together and feeding off each other in an attempt to not feel the emptiness that resides inside. Many groups of friends do the same thing to a greater or lesser extent.

As they come together they try to fill the emptiness by acknowledging only the shared values; listening to similar music; reading the same books; playing the same computer games; and they may even all communicate a great deal with each other on the Internet. Nowadays there are even cyber worlds such as one called *Second Life*. People can log in and live the type of life they want instead of dealing with the *real world*. This escape works for many. It can work like a drug, or like the zombie box, but one is still not living in reality. The reality of which I am speaking is not the reality that I speak of when I say *real world*. I am speaking of the reality that most of us have forgotten; the reality from which we were born.

As quantum scientists tell us now and mystics have been telling us forever, there is something greater that lies beyond our reality. Our realities are made up of decisions we have made. When we decided to form a certain personality, and chose what would be valuable for our lives and our survivors and what wouldn't, we started our journey on a road that we were creating as we went. **Once we constructed the foundation for our belief system that interpreted the world for us, we began to only work within the concretized structure that we thought**

was the real. The infinite possibility of paths in our brains that were active when we were babies so that we could create and live full lives shut down. The neurons in the brain that we did not use stopped firing as the thoughts and the ideas that would have been associated with their activity simply ceased.

The ideas that we contemplated and accepted as the basis for truth and reality created familiar paths for the firing of neurons. The energy began to flow with ease through paths that it utilized frequently. If we look at a field or a forest we can understand the way the paths in our brain work. If we will walk across a grass field as it grows and becomes a forest and we take the quickest easiest path, we will eventually create a rut in the earth. As the grass grows long and trees cover the field the only places left clear will be the paths that we have been walking. If we want to go somewhere, we choose the path. If we want to go another way we must cut through the undergrowth, the trees, and the tangled masses of vegetation and thorn bushes.

If we keep thinking the same things repeatedly, or using the same patterns of thoughts connected with predictable behaviors, our unused synaptic paths will begin to close down. We can go in another direction, but not without much work. It will be like cutting through the trees, the undergrowth and long grasses. Most people don't want to do that, especially when society provides the opportunity not to do so.

When we find friends who agree with us, and we agree on one culture and one way of doing things best, we solidify the paths we started when we were young. We are still working on the same paths; building on the same foundation. The very thing that helped us survive is what ends up killing our natural intelligence and our creative abilities. We begin to choke ourselves off. The more we learn from a society that worships the ego and a drive to have power-over others to prove ones worth and gain self-esteem—an ego that helps us stay in a little box it has created, the more frozen and minimalist our thinking ability becomes until we begin to bring a minimalist thinking ability to every aspect of our lives. **In the *Ego Box* we are controlled by four attachments or *S-Factors:* 1) Our *sexuality* and sexual issues; 2) our *significance*, or how important we are in the world in comparison with others; 3) our *society* or sociability, or how we fit in, in society and how likable we are; and 4) our *solitude*, or how we deal with the belief that we are individuals separate from everyone else.** Most of our lives our spent working within this prescribed box trying to find a sense of peace and balance. We can do this sometimes, but it is at the cost of keeping out anything that might challenge the ideas, correct or incorrect, that sustain this box. Some people live in this box all of their lives and never grow to become who they are.

Upon discovery of the *dark matter* in the universe and views of the world through the H*ubble Telescope*, many scientists deduced that we only perceive about 5% of reality because of our physical limitations as a species. Due to additional mental and cultural limitations that we place on ourselves as a species, we see less than 1%. In that case, they say, ESP, communication with animals, energy work, auras, and many other things in the universe are a distinct possibility.

Joining together with friends or with families that support our belief systems and the personality that we have chosen seems like a good thing. It takes away some of the emptiness, sometimes, and helps us feel relaxed and pleased. We constantly look for places where we are accepted as we are and sometimes friends provide us with such opportunities. **The problem is that we are often just reinforcing our acceptance of who people have told us that we are, and not who we really are. We are reinforcing the little strip of an infinite mind called the ego and saying "this is me." In reality the ego is not who we are. The ego is a set of ideas, rules, laws, and judgments assembled by the infant mind to make sense of a scary world. The infant must adapt to survive. The ego becomes the necessary adaptation tool in an imperfect world.**

Once it has done its job we can let go of it. Once we know the rules of this world and how to apply them, and how survive on this planet, we can let go of the ego identity and be who we really are—part of this greater, living entity called the universe, or God. But this is easier said than done because the ego wants to carry out the order given it at the time of its creation; it wants to live so its host can live, and it wants to give its host the power to conquer the world and to freeze time so that it is comfortable.

If one was in a beautiful loving place when the ego was developed it would have frozen time and space as a healthy environment. All of our thoughts and behaviors toward other people and ourselves would serve to recreate a healthy atmosphere and environment so we would stay in the same place. This would only happen, however, if ones parents were enlightened and treated one as the expansive, divine being that she truly was. If we were in a troubled place of frightening place when the ego was developed, as most of us were, the ego would help us recreate that frightening, horrible place over and over throughout our lives; it will continue to do so if we don't break free of its influences. The object of the ego is to keep everything in the environment the same so that it can master the environment. This is what is known of as karma.

Karma does not come from a hateful universe that wants to punish us, it comes from who we are. It comes from the behaviors of the ego and the censor that were developed to create stability in the life of an infant who was an infinite being who only knew peace and stability before it took on a human body. Since karma is linked to the ego and the censor, the only way to be free of it is through transformation of the ego and the destruction of the censor. When we can shatter the censor we can transform the ego by dispelling the energy needed to freeze it and hold it together. As the ego returns to the supra ego, or the higher consciousness and bearer of earthly and heavenly wisdom, we can release Atman, the true divine self.

There is then no need for the ego, only for living a full, beautiful, creative life. This, however, cannot be done by finding a group of friends that agree with us, or by being counter-cultural or oppositional; it can only be done by doing the inner-work; It can only be done through following the path of the *warrior mystic*. One needs to have the will, desire, and intention to dismantle every false belief system until one comes to what is real. Hanging around with friends who claim to create a culture that is counter to a culture of illusion while creating yet another more invisible culture that is also an illusion will not lead to life; it will only lead to more disillusionment and blindness. Unfortunately, we don't usually realize this until we are older. When we leave home and go to college, the service, or take on the requirements of being an adult we usually see that our counter- cultural lives were an illusion and that we were often more reactionary and closed off than the culture we despised.

Unfortunately, in some cultures this never happens. One's success at staying in a paradise with friends, families and neighbors often leads to ingrained self deception, stagnation, and internal death as one realizes that it is meaningless also. When this happens it is important to find someone else with whom to identify. Many people, though not all, often identify with the Great Teachers, or even school teachers, professors, or Sunday School teachers. They begin to identify with people who can pass on knowledge and wisdom, after they learn that the essence they thought they had through connection with their own little

33

group, was really only emptiness and not the real essence of life at all.

These are hard lessons that those who want to grow spiritually must learn. Even so, they are hard to understand because they move beyond dualism—the belief that everything exists at the two far points of a spectrum. In truth there are no end-points and sometimes what is good for you is bad for you, and what is bad for you is good for you. This is a concept that is difficult to grasp when the major part of the society's thinking and the ego's thinking depends on this artificial idea of dualism. We create a world that consists of opposites and denies the spectrum on which all things exist. We talk about up, down, in, out, right, left and good, or bad. In reality these things do not exist cleanly upon close examination.

While we are in the zombie box they exist. They have to, so we can know what to expect in the world and so that we can freeze time. They are what maintain the order of the neurons are firing in our brains that create the ruts in our thinking, but as soon as we step outside of those ruts we find a whole new world. Dualism, like the ruts, provide easy explanations for how things work; it not only does that, but promises us that we can control the world by applying one tool or the other, or one thought or the other, to any problem we have. We know what to expect and we can predict things using dualism, but all dualism is, is a creation of the human being. **It is a useful tool, but in reality it doesn't exist. The problem is that this tool of the human being, like the ego, becomes the**

master when one is not careful and begins to believe that it is real.

In school during arithmetic class, they showed us the symbol of the line in arithmetic. It was a line with an arrow on each end. Perhaps you can remember this. The line was supposed extend to negative infinity in one direction and positive infinity in the other. The same idea was represented in the circle for pre-dualistic societies. Since it was a circle one could go in any direction forever. When we look at the world we have created through dualism, we find what is known a segment of a line; it is the space between two points that we place randomly on the line. We are presented with a very small segment of reality similar to the drawing on the board, and are told that it is the only *real* that exists. .

Our eating, our sleeping, our breeding, everything that we do is done in this very small segment of reality. If we find something useful that doesn't fit into the corporate idea of reality, but it becomes popular and of worth, we, as a society, just extend reality by moving the dot at the end of the line by just a micro movement to the right. Our society declares that that little space is reality and that all we can't perceive outside of it is meaningless unless we can pull it into this little segment, bring it under the power of dualism, and use it in the material world for something.

The truth is that there is no up or down. If we point up and someone on the other side of the earth points up

we are pointing in opposite directions. The same is true if we point down. To deal with this dilemma scientist have said that pointing down meant pointing toward the center of the earth while pointing up meant pointing away from the center. If we are on the moon or another planet, however, that doesn't work. If we are in space, which is a totally infinite endless space there is no up or down, because there are no reference points except for random ones. So our dualism is only agreed upon reference points that were needed for us to be able to work in the material world and to survive as a species. A one inch nut needs a one inch wrench. In that case it has to be one inch, or not one inch. Dualism was created in order to conquer the material world and to help us feel more comfortable about being able to control our surroundings, just like the ego and the censor.

Dualism is also a tool of the superego. As long as one can define what thoughts and behaviors are good or bad, and can make people feel miserable and damned if they do not do everything on the good side, the definer has the power to control thinking and behavior. If ideas of good can be planted into our heads at a young age, and neutral thoughts and behaviors can be paired with the word *good* while others are paired with the words *bad,* we will think that we are good if we think and behave in a way that is in concert with the ones defined as good. **The superego is the internalization of good and bad paired with the words, phrases and signifiers (symbols and words that help us understand small bits of reality) that tell us if we are**

good or bad. Those signifiers, or words, are not our own. They have been planted in our minds by parents, and other authority figures, and now the media. In order to break free from the influences of the ego and superego we need to break free of dualism. The idea of good and bad must somehow be transcended. The only way that we can transcend the concepts and the need for them in order to keep order in the world is by holding together the opposites. Sitting with two opposite ideas and living in the paradox until they meld into reality is our only way to freedom and expansion of our minds and thinking capability.

Sitting in a place of paradox and expanding beyond the many syllogisms planted in our minds is what ultimately leads us to the real reality. The ultimate reality this process brings us to is a return to the being within us known as *Atman*, which is the real person—the real I. We are the reality, not dualism, or the spectrums, or the world created by the fantasies of the ego. Our reality at the center of the paradox is what pulls the artificially supported world of dualism back together into the unity of reality and life. Life is something to be lived and experienced fully without the chatter of other people's voices in our heads. We are that life. We are not separate from it.

When one is fully awakened, or enlightened, one realizes that that which is good can also be bad and that which is bad can also be that which is good. This is a deeper form of thinking. Dualism only allows us to think shallowly so that we never come to reality, or break the power of the ego. Reality exists as various paradoxes. Is it any wonder that the original word for religion, *religios* in Greek, means bending back to our origins, or bridging? As we live in the now and hold that space and our greater origins in dynamic tension something happens; we thrive in the energy of the paradox and the dynamic balance. This dynamic balance is what keeps planets, stars, and galaxies on their courses, and sustain the dynamic energy that we call life.

Without paradox being held together there is no life, only stagnation. If we live lives based on the *all-or-none-principle* where we are always striving for a feeling of well being based on having more and more, our life will be reduced to something like a cog in a machine that is active with a lot of movement, but void of love, joy, and life. Though many people in western society like to refer to us as parts of a machine and don't mind maintaining that archetype for the human family, and hope that we strive to think of ourselves non-organic beings so we'll work harder, we are not inorganic. Not identifying with nature gives us the illusions of godhood. We cut our bodies, we nip and tuck them, we work them out in order to reshape them, and if they break down the physician or psychiatrist uses a medical model that breaks us down into little parts and seeks to treat the parts, but not the whole organic being.

We now worship the inorganic: the fast car; the computer; robotics, all types of things that lift the machine and the invention of man above that which is organic. We destroy the organic so we can create something inorganic out of it. It is only of worth when it is inorganic and created by the hands of humanity to be folded into a cash and carry society. The truth is, however, that we are not biological machines, we are living organisms.

. Living in an organic world and acting like an inorganic, man-made creation is not something that most of us want after we become aware that it is happening. We want to live lives fully, to love freely, and to be truly happy. This is the nature of the human being who has not been damaged by the world, but never the nature of the one who makes his or herself into a machine to avoid the fears and the disappointments of life.

The Path of Teachers
Chapter 5

If we are not satisfied with our lives and we are living quiet lives of desperation, or just trying to "put in our time" by enjoying life until we die, we are in a desperate situation. Much of the desperation stems from the fact that we don't consciously know to expect anything better. On some level, however, if we will pay attention we can know intuitively that there is more. Our intuition and feelings can lead us to begin a search for that *better thing* without even knowing what it really is. How can we do this? How can we quicken the process that draws us to the infinite, and more importantly, what steps can we take to find the infinite?

One way that we can search for more is by identifying with someone who seems happy, knowledgeable, and well adjusted, instead of angry and disillusioned. In other words, we seek someone better off than we are. As children we find ourselves identifying with those who have more knowledge and control. This begins with our parents, but as we begin to move outward in our social network it extends to others. If our family and our friends leave us with an empty feeling, we will often begin to identify with people who are more powerful and who represent the power of the system. Since we usually go to school when we are children, except for those home schooled, this is often the teacher. Not just any teacher, however, but our favorite teacher who is one who has characteristics that we would like to nourish in ourselves.

Good teachers are a godsend, mainly because of the work they do and the affect they have on children, and because there aren't many very good ones. When one finds a good one he is as good as gold. A good teacher can take a child from the worst of circumstances, share themselves with that child, and turn her whole life around. A good teacher can change maladaptive behaviors and thought patterns that have been in a family system for generations, and affect the coming generations in new exciting ways, but this type of intervention takes time, dedication and a great deal of effort. Many teachers are often burdened with too many students to do this. They often look for the student who exhibits the most interest and talent, or the ones who have the most need. Those in the center, the "C" students, are often ignored, unless they reach out for help. A student who is bright and inquisitive, or just plain inquisitive can find a good mentor in a teacher.

Getting to know a teacher well can inspire a child to study more and get better grades. Getting better grades becomes a very powerful positive reinforcement for a child as doors open for him or her that will not open for someone with fair or poor grades. As the student studies more and sees more success, he or she experiences growth in strength, character, and resolve. From this resolve there is an increase of constancy, devotion, and perseverance in the student, as well as a sense of empowerment. It is impossible for this to be bad. It is, in fact, very good for the student and the teacher, especially in a power-over world. There is always a space for bright, inquisitive, hardworking people in a power-over world; they are the ones who support and uphold the power-over system and power-over thinking.

The only challenge for the student who is bright, inquisitive, and hardworking is the reaction of his or her peers. Being intelligent and close to a teacher, or several teachers, often engenders anger and envy from one's peers. If one chooses this path one will soon discover that it is more difficult than expected, not because one cannot get ahead, but because it separates one from close relationships with most of one's peers. Whether this is good or bad I cannot say; in the long run it can be good or bad; it depends on the choices that one makes and the type of personality that one has. As we look at the many people that were called *nerds* and *geeks* who studied hard, hung out with

41

small peer groups that supported them, and got good grades, we can see that some of them did very well. Many of those who overcame peer pressure and continued to study and work hard ended up being the bosses of the more popular ones and making great contributions to the world.

Their parents were very proud, the friends that they had were usually real friends instead of fair weather friends, and they usually ended up very well off economically. Those who weren't too damaged by the popular people torturing them often know how it is to be an outsider and learn to identify with the outsider who is often oppressed and put down. On the other side, however, there are those who were so psychologically damaged that they can never succeed. They were crippled because of the cruelty of envious peers. Many of them have even had mental breakdowns, or they have learned to strive so much to be like those cruel peers that they have lost themselves.

When I was growing up people used to pretend to be like less intelligent peers. They would go to school and do enough work to have good grades, but they would never excel and reach their full potentials for fear of drawing the wrath of their less intelligent peers. Fitting in was more important than excelling. Many of them did very well in life, but the desire to stay in the crowd and not excel was woven into their psyches and life narrative. Mediocrity became a part of their ego structures frozen there by the censor and they never really excelled. They never learned to outreach their peers and limitations and take wing. When they had the opportunity to rise up they would often sabotage themselves, subconsciously, reliving their youth and thinking they would be tortured by their peers if they excelled. They, of course, didn't realize this, because their censor was keeping it secret and under the radar of their conscious. Fitting in when they were young and holding themselves back provided comfort and safety, but the tool used to survive then, ultimately became the master and destroyed their creativity at a later age.

The ones who did well and excelled despite the envy of peers also fell into traps. They internalized their identification with the power-over structure and became authoritarian. They began to think that they had more intellectual ability and better ideas. They became the ones who would make people work for them and conform to their ideas about how their little piece of the world should be. The rejection of their peers and anyone who reminded them of their peers, the need and desire to become one of the *insiders* of the power group happened and their hearts were hardened. It was as if they filled their empty spaces by getting the acclaim that they needed from other people's praise and a power-over form of being. They gained self esteem by performing the right way like a trained, domesticated animal. Their reward ultimately became training other animals instead of having to be beasts of burden themselves. Movement from the oppressed to the oppressor was the reward for their hard work and faithfulness to the power-over system. To be successful in a dominator society one must be a dominator, no matter how kind or caring one attempts to be, but if one is harboring internalized anger, he or she is often even more oppressive than the average person.

Those who did not deal with the underlying anger and resentment begin to project the faces and the characteristics of the peers who tortured them for doing well at a young age onto others. Anyone who was in competition with them was dehumanized and seen as the enemy—the other children who had tried to come between them and their essence, or their nourishment. The rejection those people, those peers, on the subconscious level had become important for their psychic survival when they were children. Those same feelings had been imprinted in their egos and projected onto everyone with whom they came in contact as adults. Anyone who reminded them of those peers was understood as *the problem.* They were what got in the way of obtaining peace and essence. This caused the angry achievers to always fight to get rid of such people, and to think they couldn't find peace and happiness as long as those other cruel people existed. They never dealt with the real problem. The real problem was an internal one. The feelings of inferiority from the teasing was still there as a shadow. It was a shameful, empty feeling that was masked by a drive for superiority and the adoption of a supremacist, false identity.

Instead of recognizing the emptiness within themselves, the angry well adjusted achiever who was very close to the teacher projected the emptiness outside onto those peers who were unruly, while drenching themselves

**with the energy and happiness of the teachers and parents
who lauded them with praise. Their mental DNA recorded
this and the need to have it. Their lives were frozen there
and their ego, subconscious, and censor began to work in
order to recreate this situation again and again. As a result
of this they would have difficulty with their peers forever.
They would become angry authoritarian leaders who would
prove their worth by having a high place in the system and
drawing close to the power people.** This is not the case with all
children who perform well in school despite peer pressure, but it
is for many. A good relationship with teachers can be very
favorable, but it can also create thoughts, attitudes, and feelings
inside that cannot be easily resolved. If the teacher is pointing us
in the right direction by helping us remain in a balanced
relationship between time with the teacher and time with our
peers it can be life saving. If we develop a teacher vs. peer
attitude this can lead to trouble. These thoughts that diminish
peers and uphold authority figures solidify the ego more and
diminishes the possibility of the freedom which comes from
breaking free of one's ego and life narrative and returning to
one's own identity and living in the present.

**The attitude and relationships that we have with
peers are transferred onto other people, but the attitudes and
relationships that we have with teachers are also transferred
to other people who have power. We can begin to feel close to
power figures, or we can judge them wrongly because they
are not like the teacher we liked. Our super ego may even**

judge us harshly because we are not like the teacher we liked. On the opposite end, if we were one of those who didn't like our teacher, or who got tortured for getting along too well with the teacher and quickly broke off the relationship, we may project our attitudes and responses about that teacher and the whole situation onto every other teacher and authority figure. We may distrust all authority figures just because of our experience with them during our formative years. We may draw closer to our less intelligent, raucous peers and begin to dislike all authority figures. That is why it is important for us to recognize that *The Path of Teachers* for finding essence instead of emptiness, is not one that leads to the end that we desire. The path for essence through connection with the teacher in grade school, high school, or any educational institution where envy and jealousy may occur in our peers, is very difficult. There are, however, other types of teachers. There are spiritual teachers that can give us some insights. We don't often hear about those, but as time passes we hear about them more.

Since the sixties in the U.S., when the Beatles began to study yoga and Hinduism, the idea of a guru has become more popular. While this was happening, along with many psychologists experimenting with mind altering drugs and experiences, and transcendental meditation and other techniques, many westerners began to seek teachers to show them the way. This, of course, is not a new practice. Throughout the ages there have been great spiritual leaders with many followers. Many of the sacred texts of the great religions of the world have been written by or about such figures. These figures were, and are, said to be able to lead us to our true selves...our divine selves, through word and deed. Some are even said to be able to do miracles, or things that seem impossible to the average person.

There are several ways to gain access to teachers. Some people go to hundreds of workshops led by those who are said to be great, spiritual leaders. Open a catalog for some retreat centers and you can find smiling pictures of many of them with small descriptions just like the pictures of wardrobes and the newest bicycles that one would have found in a Sears Catalog in the 1800s. We can get whatever we want, if we can afford it.

Some more sober minded people seek one teacher from a very old tradition. They dedicate themselves to one path in order to obtain enlightenment, which means *being awakened*. They may then do whatever it is that enlightened people do, which is teach, work as a custodian, or just live a life of bliss. They can get their pictures put into those catalogs and travel all over the country to try to help other people come to the light.

It is said that a relationship with a teacher is very important. If the teacher is good she or he will empower you. He or she will be able to see through all of your conditioning and all of the tricks that you are playing on yourself so that you may be set free by yourself and God, not by her or him. This is a good teacher.

Some teachers, however, may not be so good. There is a lot of pressure on a teacher. The artificial need for

perfection is often projected onto them. Most teachers are not perfect, according to the consensus of everyone in the world, so they can't measure up to everyone's idea of what a teacher should be. Teachers who get trapped in a situation where they lose themselves and try to become perfect, or even really think they are, usually fall hard. This gives the unofficial judges and nay Sayers who don't agree with such beliefs the ammunition they need for an all out attack against the teacher and spirituality. Mostly, it gives them the opportunity to feed their own egos. Many people who glory in the fall of teachers and spiritual people come from the group of people who have had problems long ago with some authority figure or the other.   They, like the peers described earlier in this chapter, envy people with power, or are jealous them. **They do not experience spirituality, enlightenment, or joy because of this anger so they don't believe that it exists. They try to destroy anyone who proves that it does, because that person's existence threatens their understanding of the world and their fragile egos.**

People who experience love, truth and joy are a problem for such people. These people exhibit the very traits and characteristics they have denied and pushed aside during the formation of their ego and censor. They have pushed all of these traits and characteristics down into what Carl Jung describes as the *shadow*. The shadow is a conglomeration of thoughts and behaviors that are being held down below the conscious. They are the thing that we needed to get rid of to

form our own unique personalities. When we see a person who has all of those traits and living happy and joyful lives we begin to question whether we did the right thing on a subconscious level. Such questions may cause all of the repressed feelings to rise. This would cause our ego to expand and transform to the point where it would die as it was and become something new. The censor wants to protect the ego from that so the censor blocks the information by making us angry and filling us with resentment. It makes us want to see these people and anyone like them fail. When they do we are happy because that person is not a threat to us anymore. Our false world is left intact.

When we meet a person that just pushes all of our buttons for no reason, it is likely that we are looking at our shadow in that person. What is necessary for healthy, psychological growth and spiritual growth is to embrace our shadow and to learn to understand it. When we do this all of the energy used to hold down all of those traits will slowly be released and we will have that energy available for life and spiritual transcendence again. The irony is that the target of our anger and envy, the very teacher that we may not like and the ideas that we may not like are the ones that can teach us to use that energy as it is slowly released. We are, therefore, cutting off our own hand to spite the rest of our body.

It is important to recognize the power dynamics influencing our lives, and how what is happening in society on the outside is being transferred to the inside. It is also important to realize how what is on the inside of us shapes what is on the outside—the larger society. We work hard to try to understand a complex world in simple ways. We come up with quick shallow answers and accept them because they are easy and because they feel comfortable. We don't do this on purpose; we don't have a choice. **The ego that we set up to freeze time and provide comfort is just following its commission as we end up living a life of fantasies. The ego, along with the censor and our own Karma, are following our orders. They are doing what we wanted when we were very young. They are doing what we, with our divine creative energy, created them to do.**

The problem is that they have taken on lives of their own. We can no longer control the ego and it can no longer control the censor. The ego, which is controlled itself, controls us to the point that we think we are it. It is as if some alien force called the ego has taken over our bodies and we are just going along for the ride, but unable to control the steering wheel. If we learn how to control it the censor will simply block out the realization and make us forget how we learned to break free in a few days, and then we will end up going in the same direction as before. We will be living the same occurrences repeatedly in different places and with different people, and we will make sure that the same outcome will happen. That outcome will be what was happening when we wrote messages on our ROM (Read Only Memory). This ROM is the ego.

A spiritual teacher can help us to erase our ROM, but only if she is willing and able to get passed all of our maladaptive defense mechanisms and show us how to dismantle the ego. This won't happen unless the teacher is very adept and talented, and we are honest and willing enough to struggle with our own projections onto that teacher. **If we aren't careful the censor will just get us to reject that teacher so we won't change. It can even make us choose a teacher that will help us hold onto our same attitudes while thinking we are moving closer toward enlightenment. We will be strengthening the ego that we are trying to dismantle.**

The Path of the Teacher can lead us to truth and light, but on that path we must always be observant. We must be observant of our relationship with the teacher as well as our relationship with our peers and our families. Somehow, in the midst of all of this work, we need to create enough balance to assure us that we are not pulling too far away from any one influential group. At the same time, however, we must be willing to give up any group that may keep us on the road of illusion and threaten our happiness and success in this world as well as in the world of the spirit. The desire of most human beings who have reached a high enough state of spiritual evolution is to become enlightened; **it is to be fully awake and to have complete access to communion with God and to experience the bliss of God in this world, in our physical bodies, as well as in the world to come. When we are awake heaven will be wherever we go. Dying will just be passing from one heaven to another.**

The Path of Danger
Chapter 6

It would be great if everyone could find a great spiritual teacher, but who has time for that? I'm afraid very few. Most people have to work forty plus hours to be able to make a living. Everyone can't leave their family, friends or their job to go on a spiritual search for truth. Many people in the west would even call such a quest irresponsible, or say they are avoiding reality. We learn that we have a duty to our friends and family to be the best that we can. Being the best is usually associated with the type of jobs we have and how much money we make, or at least how much control we have over others. Since this is often the case in western civilization, it is no wonder, taking these factors into account, that most people do not do it.

Many people resort to going to workshops, since they can't afford to go off on a quest and find a teacher. The problem with this is that many of the workshops are very expensive. A lot of money spent going to workshops could be used for food, clothing, car payments, and insurance. How can the head of a family possibly excuse using all that money or time working with a spiritual teacher? Some people just can't, or they never consider it. Many people choose a different path that can seem to fill the emptiness-- *The Path of Danger*. This path is more acceptable in western society and it is free from any religious baggage.

One need not be religious or spiritual to choose the path of danger. In fact, many who choose this path are neither. **Many people who choose the path of danger are seeking peace and the power of their essence through destructive behavior by putting themselves in danger to feel the thrill of life. They are dead at the center and can only feel emotions by going overboard and doing too much. As they do dangerous things, increasingly, they begin to need more and more of an adrenaline rush just to feel normal.** When they don't have that rush they begin to feel everything else, including the emptiness and grief they have never dealt with. Instead of dealing with it by facing the grief and the fear, they choose to fill the emptiness with drugs, adrenaline packed activities, dangerous sexual activities, or other such practices. The only thing that all these practices have in common is that they are dangerous and the take the person off the path to truth, enlightenment, and inner-healing.

It is as if the empty person is looking for an acceptable way to commit suicide. They are forcing themselves to feel something other than pain and emptiness. As long as they get away with their thrill seeking lives they never have to face the emptiness. As long as they are climbing every mountain, or jumping out of airplanes, or snowboarding down dangerous slopes they don't have to feel. Others see them as exciting, active people, **but most mental health professionals can readily see that they have what they call a *death-wish*.** The path of danger does not lead to divine union, only a numbing of the inner self.

53

This numbing doesn't last long enough. As soon as the person becomes quiet he realizes that he is in pain and suffering.

The only thing that can possibly help this person attain the true essence of life is often injury. It is coming to a point where she can't perform all of these destructive acts. This causes the same type of withdraw symptoms that a drug addict usually has. That is because in this case this type of behavior is no more than a drug. It seems as though it is an *upper*, but what it really does is sedate a person so he or she never really has to go into the center and explore the emptiness. **This emptiness is always there waiting for a time to express itself. Whenever the person's guard is down it will rise up, because it is still there. It is always there. It is necessary to enter into the emptiness and deal with it for that type of person and any person to have a fulfilled, healthy life.**

The unprocessed grief is manifest through inappropriate behavior for this person. One might project one's anger, sadness, and numbness onto others, because she doesn't want to experience them. They don't just disappear. She can see the world as an empty place, or see individuals as worthless beings because they are not as adept at risking their lives as she. She may hate people who play it safe, as she makes their behavior into her own internal shadow. The one thing that she needs to save herself is rejected as she goes deeper and deeper into a well of destruction.

People trapped in this mode of behavior often hit bottom hard. This hitting the bottom can result in irreparable

mental damage, chronic disease, or even death, or suicide. There
is nothing like having to start living from the bottom and having
to try to climb up from a hole with a social disease that cannot be
healed, or a string of children, or with a mental health problem.
Such injuries can easily occur with people who take the path of
danger.

I know a lot of people who took that path. Earlier I
mentioned the town in which I was raised. It was a small city,
but booming economically for a time, before hard times. As it
got worse the neighborhoods got worse. They imported gang
members and drug pushers in from some poor neighborhood
through the welfare system and section eight housing. Soon our
little neighborhood became a neighborhood infested with drug
addicts, drug pushers, prostitutes, and gangs. The businesses
began to flee as more and more of them were getting robbed.
Houses were being broken into. Anyone who could afford to
quickly fled. I would attribute this to what some people refer to
as *white flight*, but many of the African American fled too. The
only ones that didn't, didn't have the means.

Several of the less violent, more adjusted children
and families were trapped living in what had become a *concrete
jungle.* Some escaped by working hard and going to college.
Some survived long enough to graduate High School and go to
the army. Some people just stayed there and worked at any
menial job they could find, or got on welfare. They began to
smoke or use drugs to deaden the pain of being trapped in this
living hell with no hope of escape. Most of them ended up

committing suicide, carrying out behaviors that got them killed, or going to the mental hospital. Instead of illegal drugs they were given prescription drugs to ease the pain, and told they would have to stay on those drugs forever. Why not? Many of them were using drugs for the same reason before they became mentally decapitated.

The path of danger always brings about death and destruction. It kills one's hopes and dreams. It kills one's ability to go inside to find the truth, and to find one's own identity. It numbs one so much that he can no longer feel; he can no longer feel pain, but he can also no longer feel love. This, I think, is the *abomination of desolation* that was predicted in the *Book of Daniel* that reduces whole civilizations to waste. This is something that takes place in the ghettos and barrios all over the world for those who are not careful, or who do not have wise parents or teachers. This is a living death--a living hell. It is the type of hell that extends after one's life on this earth to the next life, because there is really only one life. We take what we are-- the way we have created ourselves, from one existence to the next. **If we do not do the work necessary to free ourselves, to burn off the karma and to awaken as Atman which dwells within, we will journey through life and many lives in a school that is repeatedly trying to teach us the same lesson.**

We will be trapped in a downward spiral. The same situations will present themselves to us repeatedly in life. The faces and locations will change, but we will still be the same. Our censor and our subconscious will keep

supplying us with the same lesson by putting us in the same situations until we get the message and reach out and grab our freedom. Some call this hell. Some people will call it the worst curse ever and curse God for such actions. In reality, however, this is a great blessing. **The God that we are cursing is actually our divine Self, the one who helps set up these situations so we will be awakened, we will be reawakened to our own greatness if we finish the course successfully, or wake up when given the opportunity repeatedly. All of the fear, the anger, and the temptations that so easily beset human beings will fade away right now, in this lifetime, if we heed the lessons. We will become masters of our fate instead of followers as we do Sat Yoga, burning off all of the karma from past lives and this life. As we remove these behavioral tracks, or *sanskara*, we become whole and free and live as the light of the world.**

Living a dangerous life becomes foolish. We realize that we are eternal beings. Life and death don't exist anymore. We become fearless as yogis and begin to live a life of perfection. **We become the light of the world, or the city on the hill that cannot be hidden as our love, beauty, kindness, and patience shine like a beacon in a dreary world. This only takes place if we dare to take the only truly frightening journey: the inner journey.**

When we begin to look at ourselves and look at all of the pain that we have suffered and not turn away, and look at all of the pain we have caused and not turn away, we will

see that we are living an illusion. We will realize that we have created a false life with false meaning, and that all that we have that we thought was the best is meaningless. All the times we fought to achieve; all of the bank accounts that we have; all of the material things, or women or men that we have adoring us are meaningless. All of the trophies and plaques become simply peaces of wood, glass, and metal as we realize that the only important thing is basking in essence that dwells within. When we have the essence we have it all. When we have the essence we have God and we realize that we are part of that One being and that we are all part of each other. Our separation becomes an illusion as we reclaim our divinity and live as the Gods that we were meant to be. This only happens when the ego is put to death and that divine spark, the true self, is allowed to live and flourish.

In just about any worthy religion there is a concept of death and resurrection. Someone dies and descends to the underworld. The divine power lifts that person from the depths of the underworld to heaven, and then when the person returns to earth, or wherever they return, they are a new, transformed being. They have become their true selves like a phoenix rising from the ashes or a butterfly breaking out of a cocoon.

When we have transformed our egos the small "I" dies, it is put to death in the underworld and then the Atman, the divine power, lifts it up and transforms it. It is dead, but it lives as something else, like a seed broken and creating new life. The resurrection story is not just about some other person; it is the spiritual journey we all must take if we want to live. This is the truly frightening journey. This is the *path with heart* that leads to eternal life, not riding down the hill on a board. After having a very destructive dangerous life, many people who have been on the Path of Danger, begin to seek this path through religion and spirituality.

To Obtain Freedom
Section 3

The Path of Religion
Chapter 7

Several religions are famous for seeking out people who are down and out—at the bottom of themselves, finding them, and then converting them to their religion, which happens to be superior to every other one. There are missionaries all over the world from various religious sects: Born Again Christians, Mormons, Jehovah Witnesses, Masonic Jews, Seventh Day Adventists, Hare Krishna's, and even some Buddhists nowadays, go out and seek individuals to bring them to the light. The promise of many of these religions is salvation. This salvation may take place in several different ways, but the ultimate end is to make it to something—some place, where all pain and suffering ends.

Most of these religious converts meet in some type of group where they seek to create their own culture. In most instances these groups are counter-cultural, in that they do not agree fully with the *way of the world*. Many of them see this world as nothing but an illusion, or as something accursed from which we must escape. They follow a charismatic religious leader usually, and have some teachings that have been passed down from that leader that provide insights and techniques that will help one transcend the self, and the world.

Some promise freedom from the wheel of reincarnation to dedicated followers, while some guarantee that the true believer will escape hell and go straight to heaven. Along with this bonus they will also have kinship with God and be able to draw on miraculous powers to perform healings and miracles. Some of them uphold the examples of great teachers who have somehow gained enough power or insight to do miracles that transcend the laws of physics and say that we can all do this. All of theses paths can be very seductive. The groups, or the collectives associated with them, can be very seductive too. These groups supply the ego with the love that it never received during its formation and possibly throughout childhood.

If one has a bad parent image one can re-parent oneself by connecting with a God, Goddess, or Spirit that is neither male or female, or a concept that is not any being at all— only a loving presence. This gives one the unconditional love necessary to grow into a healthy, spiritual being in a world that usually doesn't support this outcome. Throughout our lifetimes, especially during formative years, being spiritual, loving, kind, and generous is often supported in word, but not in deed. As very young children we are told to be loving, kind, gentle and to share things; at the same time we are taught to be competitive, and that we are better than those who cannot beat us in our endeavors. We are often taught at a deeper level through the media and well meaning but brainwashed parents, that we are better than those who have less than us. Some of these beliefs and values are included in the religious beliefs that our parents and the greater society hold true. Many religions teach us that we will receive a lot because we are being blessed by God, thus, by the process of elimination they imply that those who have less are not receiving because they are not blessed by God.

In these religions we, like the prophet Job, are told that suffering comes from lack of wisdom, or because of some hidden evil or sin. We are told that God and the universe are good, so if we receive pain, suffering and torment it is because we are not aligned with God. We are evil in this scenario. The suffering is our problem and not God's. When we straighten out we won't suffer anymore. This is the message that the author debunked in the Book of Job when God appeared to Job and said that Job was right, he was sinless and being punished for nothing.[6] None-the-less deep in the recesses of our minds we still believe that every problem has a cause. If we can't find that cause anywhere outside we look for it inside and if we can't find it there we make it up out of superstition.

Most religions were developed by sages and mystics to set the human soul free by debunking all of the ideas of a wrathful, manlike God and focusing on a direct connection with a loving God, but there is a tendency for those who get into positions of power to change the teachings of the mystic into beliefs that reflect modern day society and modern day belief systems which vary from culture to culture. The counter-cultural

63

religion eventually becomes a religion that freezes culture and supports the dominant culture that it depends on for survival. That is what often happens to ideas and ways of life that become institutionalized.

When a person or a group of people find a good idea they try to find a way to preserve it so that it can contribute something to the world. They want to benefit from it, and they want it to survive because it has something that will help continuous generations prosper. In religious circles they are more dedicated to this because they think they have found *The Truth*. Some religious organizations feel they have the only truth, some think they have the best truth, some think they just have one truth. Usually, however, as the institution changes and the group who started it slowly die out something happens: Those who want power and who want to be esteemed begin to move into the power hierarchy.

The open minded, enlightened leaders are pushed out or replaced by religious people. These religious people follow the letter of whatever rules and laws are central to the institution, in public, anyway. They begin to forget that the most important thing is reaching union with God, and living as a loving being as a result of that connection. Instead they will begin to follow laws, rules, and principles that approximate the behaviors of love, as they see it. This is where the cultural influence comes in. What they understand as loving, kind, and good is usually only good for them, or their own little group. It has very little to do with universal good, or God.[7] People who strive to move into places of power have the strongest egos. This is the problem. The more they live by the laws and rules they press onto others the more pride they have and the bigger their egos become.

When people are elected or selected to run these institutions the ones who can follow these rules and look like they are loving are usually the ones put in charge. They have to be politically savvy, of course, so they are often cunning and willing to say what is necessary to climb to the top. They are loving and kind to people who look the way they do and act the way they do, anyone else is seen as lacking something, or not being as loving. This makes the people in the institution focus on looking like kind, loving people instead of being kind, loving people. They only need to look like kind, loving people in their own assemblies, while they can treat people outside of their assemblies, or the ones who are not like them or who have no power-over them, badly. The institution becomes tainted as those who think that they are loving because of their behavior, but who really are not because of their hardened hearts, move into positions of power and set the course for the institution.

From the outside this is very visible, but to those on the inside it is not. They have bought into the institution and its preservation so much that they will overlook the corruption. The institution has taken on a life of its own. At first it was designed with a core idea that was created to serve the people and enhance the opportunity for union with God. Within the institution there were ways to change things. It often took time and effort, but one could correct small problems as they came up and affect change in the whole. Once the institution became alive those in the center held onto enough power to not permit change. They became the egos of the institution as it took on a life of its own, and the members of the institution began to serve the institution instead of the idea at the core.

When this occurs most of the expended energy is used to support the little power group at the top and the institution, just as in the mind and body most of the energy begins to be used to support the ego. This lack of vital energy allows people to become brainwashed so they cannot see all of the covert behaviors that are in opposition to the idea that created the institution. If anyone challenges the covert behaviors they become the shadow of the institution as every negative thought and idea is projected onto that person like a scapegoat and they are socially crucified, or cast out until they come back in line and don't tell the truth.

After a while the corporate ego of the institution, the inner group, can't maintain their behavior without being able to rationalize it and make it seem good. This is when the little ego group develops what is known as the censor. Earlier we spoke of the censor as part of the mind that works to block out information from the ego. Just as we, as children, develop the ego in the last ditch effort to get some stability as soon as we become verbal beings, the ego grabs information from outside and puts aside a part of itself called the censor. The censor blocks out all contradictory information so the ego can keep moving in the one direction that it is used to and comfortable with, even if the situation is horrible and painful.

While doing Sat Yoga Shunyamurti Robert Shubow focuses on purifying the ego. When the ego is purified and stronger, it can break free from the censor. This purification of the ego is referred to as a transformation of the ego. After the transformation of the ego, and transcendence of the ego to being guided by the Supra Ego which is also knows and the Bhuddi, or Higher Intelligence, the Atman, or the divine self, is brought into union with the ego. The ego dissolves into the Atman and the divine being that we all are is alive, or resurrected. This divine being is connected directly with God, because this Atman is God. **Only a trace of the ego remains, like the ashes of a burned rope, so that we can interact with people in Maya, the plane of existence in which we live as spirits having a sensual experience.**

In the institution we need to work the same way. If we can strengthen the leadership by purifying it, and then have healthy leadership, the leadership will destroy the censor, which in this case is the covert behavior that destroys anyone who speaks the truth and pushes out all ideas that will heal the institution. When this behavior is gone and the leadership becomes strong, new thoughts and ideas begin to transform the leadership until it is open to the power of Atman, or the divine. The power of the divine through the spirit of God and through the power of the higher ideals that brought about the institution reinvigorates it, turning the leaders into the divine servants as the

Atman, the spirit in the institution that is part of God, begins to lead the institution. When that happens the leaders won't matter, because the institution will be healthy and will be moved by the power of God, just as when it began. Unfortunately, the above process doesn't often occur, especially in religious institutions.

When a person has been damaged by the world and is at the bottom of herself, she can cling to the idea of a loving community so tightly that her ego will over look anything. She will meld into the larger culture of the institution allowing it to replace her own ideals until she becomes as hypocritical as the institution and as hostile to anyone who tries to change it as the leadership. When this happens the person is lost. They are seeking *essence* again, but are finding more emptiness. Instead of finding love, peace, refuge, and meaning they find lack of meaning. This, of course, is not the case with all religious institutions. Some people find essence through religion. Many of the religious practices in healthy settings can lead one to freedom and strengthen the ego enough to override censor occasionally, but as long as the ego is still there and hasn't been transformed and later transcended, the person is still trapped in the illusion. He still needs to do the work of purifying the ego and the lower wants and desires of *the flesh,* as it is referred to in many religious traditions.

If the lower nature and the ego are not dealt with correctly, the old censor will just change and become a new one that will be aligned with the religion. There will still be a sense of emptiness, because the sensor will be maintaining it in a different way. Somewhere in the back of the mind the supra-conscious or supra-ego knows that their little loving community and their happiness and acceptance in that community is not real. It is a sham and it is still illusion Eventually emptiness takes the place of the essence again and the person struggles to avoid the emptiness.

Many experiments were done on animals that were behavior modified. If you had a dog scratch himself and you gave him a pellet of food he would scratch himself again. This could go on for quite a bit of time until the dog knew that he would get that pellet every time he scratched himself. If you ignored him he would continue to scratch and wait. After a while he would scratch himself harder with more frequency, expecting that pellet. This can be compared so a person going to a vending machine that doesn't work. The person puts in his coin and hits the button. If nothing comes he hits it harder a couple of times and then hits the coin return button. If he doesn't get his food or the coin he often bangs on it more rapidly for a few moments and the gives up. The dog does the same thing, but every once and a while long after it has stopped doing the behavior the dog will still scratch the same way still looking for that pellet.

When a religious zealot *hits the wall*, as I call it, the same things happens. In this case she will go deeper into the religion sometimes by going to more services, praying more, fasting, or whatever it takes to hold onto the essence and drive out the emptiness. She may give up and leave that religion and then go from one religion to the next trying to avoid the emptiness. This is usually what happens, eventually. She can put off this feeling of emptiness for a while, but ultimately it will catch up with her. If she refuses to choose a better, more sensible path, or enter into the emptiness completely, until she finds the bottom of it and herself, the sense of loss can become great enough to lead to mental death, or suicide, or living in a horrible state of depression if she gives up on her religious beliefs, so she most likely won't. **The problem is that she never learned that the emptiness and the essence are the same. When one explores the emptiness, completely, through the process of meditation, one finds the essence.**

Emptiness is an illusion just as the world and all of our beliefs and rationalizing are illusions that have been created and supported by our ego. The external world is an extension of our egos into a *corporate ego*. We must break through the illusion by entering into the darkness and emptiness. In the darkness we will need to face our deepest fears. We will find ourselves in a deep well where we are alone and separated from everyone. This is the Dark Night of the Soul of which St. John of the Cross spoke, where there is a sense of being alone. There is no sense of God, or hope. All of the illusions and belief systems that we learned from others don't work anymore. They all collapse and there we are left face to face with our true selves and the Divine Spirit. Not the idea of the Divine Spirit we have been given, but the true essence of God and the universe. This journey is known as *via negativa and via creativa* in the four tenants of creation spirituality as purported by

70

Dr., Rev., Mathew Fox. There are basically four vias, or paths that are constantly taking place. They do not necessarily happen in order, or neatly. One can be on two different paths in different areas or roles of life at the same time. The four paths are: 1) *Via Postiva;* 2) *Via Negativa;* 3) *Via Creativa;* 4) *Via Transformativa.* We will discuss the four paths briefly below.

Via Positiva

Via positiva, or the positive path, takes place naturally when a person is at rest. When a person doesn't have worries he is stable, relaxed, at rest, and balanced. He can see the world in a balanced way, understanding that there are some positive experiences and negative ones, but overall the world is good and friendly.

The nature of the universe, despite what many people experience, is often pleasant and peaceful when we are free of the pains of the past and worries for the future, living in the now. Usually the worry that accompanies the need to struggle to compete and reach the top, cloud our perceptions. Living gets confused with life. Living is taking on the code of behavior given us by others in this system, and doing everything that one does as a result of adhering to that code. One can stray from the code every so often, but prisons, insane asylums, and shunning serve to bring us back into it one way or the other. Life, however, is existence; it is being, not doing. When we are still enough to just be and to work out of a sense of being instead of striving, we are in harmony with nature and the celestial universe.

We are free when we can be instead of do. Being and realizing the peaceful nature of existence is the path of via positiva.

Via Negativa

Via negativa is not often pleasurable because it involves change and discomfort.   Some internal or external occurrence takes place and shakes a person out of via positiva and her sense of well-being. The person is challenged and cannot easily return to a state of balance and comfort. She is in pain and cannot find any way to attain healing. Via negativa is *the dark night of the soul.* She realizes that she is alone. There is a deep depression and a lack of the presence of any type of God or goodness in the world. One goes down to the bottom of oneself as she realizes that the things that she believed about the world are not true, or at least were very inaccurate. She is then left alone and broken.

Via negativa is the path of letting go. It is the path most necessary for spiritual and mental growth. It cleanses one of false ideas and strips the ego and the mind of the lies and illusions planted there. When we are left with ourselves we find that we are face to face with the real God. This God is our Atman—the part of ourselves that the censor and ego have been hiding. The pain and suffering breaks the power of the ego and censor. It is our opportunity for salvation. If we process things correctly during via negativa, the hidden parts of our subconscious float up to the conscious mind as we break away some of the *sanskara* (patterns of thinking and behaviors left from previous lives and previous experiences) and the fantasies of the ego. We feel lighter and more whole, like new individuals. We never grow and never break free of the ego and censor if we keep trying to flee the via negativa.

In our society we are often taught that discomfort is bad. Most of the driving force of western civilization comes from the fact that most of the creators of this civilization didn't want to be uncomfortable. Much of our housing, our transportation, our appliances, clothing, and more, were invented just to keep us from being physically uncomfortable. As a result of this, the major thing that we always want is to avoid discomfort. Since mental discomfort and fear can cause physical discomfort, we don't want that either so we build boxes around our minds so that the world will seem more predictable. More than that, in modern days, we not only want to avoid discomfort, we want to seek pleasure. We want to find a way to fix every problem and balance it out so we can return to comfort as soon as possible. **It is only by staying with the discomfort, however, or with this emptiness, that we find the essence. Avoiding the emptiness leads to eternal illusion and death, entering into the darkness fully leads to freedom and life. It is only by losing our illusory life and through the death of the ego that we gain real life. It is important not to avoid the emptiness. It is important to enter into it with a guide that can lead us and let us know what to expect. This person can only be someone**

who has traversed the dark night of the soul and has been resurrected.

Via Creativa

After one is finished with the via negativa the via creativa process, or the path of creativity, takes place. All of the pain and suffering seems to disappear. The self expands as it is reborn as one comes to term with the pain and suffering and one lets go of the parts that don't function anymore. When one goes through this process, one realizes that the external circumstances are not necessarily causing him pain, internal occurrences are. The pain and suffering are coming more from the internal reaction than the external occurrence. This is not to say that painful things don't happen. That would be ridiculous.

The truth is that many of us would love to think that we can prevent horrible things from happening in our lives, but sometimes we can't. When horrible occurrences enter our lives, all that we can often control, if we have the skill, is our reaction to them. The Greek concept of crises is one of opportunity, or a movement toward making a decision. It is represented by arriving at a fork in the road. In this scenario one must choose to go one way or another. One cannot continue to float along repeating the same old comfortable behaviors, or building on the same old thought and behavioral patterns that she had become comfortable with. She must move in a new direction. She must choose the road that leads to her goal. What is the goal of the human being? There are several, but to make it simple I will discuss it in dualistic terms, since dualism need not be abolished, just removed from the alter as the God of truth.

According to the Sat Yoga perspective, the choices that we often have are choosing emptiness, or essence. Emptiness and essence can look the same to the untrained eye, but in this case emptiness is choosing what is popular in our society. This means taking the easy road, and doing what is familiar. The strange thing is that the easy road is not always easy. The easy road can be fraught with danger. It can demand us to give up our lives, hopes and dreams, or at least postpone them, until we gain something that will give us esteem in the sight of our society and in our own minds.

In our culture it means climbing the ladder of success. This can seem like essence, because it provides us with monetary goods. In a power-over society money can buy us many things: It can give us a modicum of freedom from the society; It can remove worry by promising us food, clothing and shelter; It can open many doors and provide us the opportunity to travel, to study with teachers, and to do just about anything for which we can afford to pay. **This looks very much like the essence, or the true meaning in life. It looks like what we came to the earth for—the fulfillment of the self by climbing as high as we can on this earthly plane. The problem is that it is not essence, it is emptiness. Having all of the material things that we can, and being esteemed by others for what we have or what we do and not for who we really are on the inside, is like a hell on earth. The only thing worse is** forgetting who we are during the process of climbing the ladder and becoming an abuser on many levels and a hater of truth.

The other road that we can choose, the essence, looks different than the wide road to emptiness. It usually doesn't look as good. Sometimes it looks like a hard painful climb. It is the one where we have to drop off many things that are just too heavy to carry, especially the esteem that is given to us by others. We have to let go of all of the thoughts and ideas that we internalized that were given to us. We let go of ideas about what is good and bad as we deep inside to find what is truly good or bad for ourselves and in *our own* opinions.

As we journey on this road of essence we will find that we are going deeper into emptiness until we finally realize that there is no emptiness, only the journey. We realize that the journey is that which is most important. The journey and how we behave and live during the journey is the same as the destination. The journey is essence and the emptiness for one who has awakened from the dream of Maya. The emptiness and essence are one and the same and that the emptiness is God; the emptiness inside of us is the power that creates love, truth, and life. When we have entered into the emptiness completely we have found the end of all religion. We have found God. We have found that we are really the essence of God and then we unravel the ego.

The necessity to choose a direction at the fork in the road comes as a result of passing through via negativa into via creativa. **If we choose the path of emptiness called Maya, which looks like essence, we will continue to live a dualistic, unfulfilled life and continue to cycle through the paths of creation spirituality. If we choose the path of essence, which looks like emptiness, (lack of Maya) we will move beyond dualism and be catapulted up out of this whole system of pain and suffering, and become our divine selves. We will be transformed into the essence of love.** We will be on the path of via transformativa, or the path of transformation where we realize that we are the emptiness, we are the essence, we are the love for which we are searching and we have the power to live as love—an applied love that can transform the world.

Via Transformativa

Via transformativa, the path of transformation is taken as we become new beings. We have talked about following these four paths in life and overcoming obstacles that take place in diverse life experiences one by one, but we can actually become transformed human beings and end all of the pain, suffering, and disillusionment that we experience rapidly, during our lives here on Earth. During the moment of via transformativa, if it is an internal process, we are set free.

Our ego, the identity that we have learned to think of as the real self, can be transformed. The negative ego is passed into the flame and the positive ego and the supra-

77

conscious, breaks free from the power of the censor and we see life as it is. The truth is no longer hidden. We are free to make choices about our lives and experience the world and creation as it is. This is like resurrection, after death. We come back as new creations.

The Atman is revived and soon the ego, which was created by us as children to take control and keep us safe, merges with the true Divine Self (Atman). It becomes the creative, fiery energy that it was in the beginning, instead of an identity that we have frozen in time and space, and we are free. We know who we are. We know who God is. We know that we are like God and that we are God now, not when we get to heaven. All of the illusion is gone, and we are free.

Helping us pass through these paths is the responsibility of any true religion or philosophy, but most of them are so trapped in the illusion that they support it, instead of unmasking it. They take the secrets that would give us life and change them to support this illusion in which we live known as Maya, by ignoring the movement of the spirit and the value of becoming mystics who *live in, move in, and have their being in God*, as the Apostle Paul said. We are lead up the hill until the culture of the religion instead of the power of the religion to transform us becomes more important.

If we become to spiritual or mystical than the church leaders who need to maintain the existence of their institution in the midst of Maya, we are often discouraged and forced to be quit or leave. The church, as an institution, is trapped if its first

78

necessity is to survive in a power position in the land of Maya, for one can only do this by using the tools of Maya. When we use the tools of Maya our censor and ego lead us to believe, once again, that Maya is real and Heaven, or God exists somewhere way out there.

As long as we think of Maya as the real world we only live on a band of reality; those who run most of our religious institutions end up living on the same little band. Their experiences have created a grid on which they base their reality. Every experience and every truth is passed through that grid like a stencil that creates and recreates an internal reality based on false understandings and expectations, until that which is love, truth and justice becomes conditional love truth and justice that is based on power-over. One is lost when his view of love, truth, and justice becomes a guise for a power-over based theology where we force our opinions onto others for *their own good.*

We are often tempted to mimic the external, western society, because there is a direct correlation between the external world that we have created corporately, and our internal landscape. We have internalized the external reality so much that we are continually recreating it. We cannot be free, because we are in feedback loop where the external illusion is constantly feeding the internal illusion and vice versus. It is necessary for us to find a religion or philosophy to break the feedback loop. That is what the via negativa and discomfort does for us if we are willing to remain in the place of discomfort. It is not comfort, therefore, that frees us, it is overcoming discomfort by transcending both comfort and discomfort.

The Force of Maya
Chapter 8

In the Hindu tradition it is said that Maya is the power of the God Vishnu to maintain order and control in the human world. Maya is but an illusion, but human beings' belief in its existence and the rightness of it makes them slaves to the forces of Maya as if it really exists. Maya is basically the world, as seen through the eyes of human beings and the system. It is the physical thing that many scientists consider reality--the only meaningful reality. In contrast to this, they considered that which is outside of Maya—the eternal truth and reality.

In the west all that is outside of the material world, or that which cannot be brought into the realm of human beings and used for the good of human beings, is of little concern. It must be able to be marketed...bought and sold, to be of worth in our consumer driven society. To Hindus the deep truths outside are what is real. The material is only used to support the body so one can connect with the true selves. According to the Mayan Indians in Central and South America the word Maya had a different, but similar meaning. Maya was not an illusion, the illusion was the idea of separation. The illusion was that this

80

material world was separate from the spiritual world. In reality all was God and God was all. Realizing this and learning to move in, live in, and breath in God was the object of life for the Mayans. Several Mayans believe that these words have similar meaning because there was contact between the Proto-Indians in India, and the Mayans in Central America. They understand the Hindu Concept as a misinterpretation of the original teaching.

In reality the Mayan idea reflects the ideals of the Yogis and one of the core beliefs of Sat Yoga. **All things are part of Brahman, the all powerful, unknowable being who is the creator of all things, and one day everyone and everything will return to Brahman. If you would like to break free from this Maya it is important to begin to explore it and see how it really works. As long as we don't explore it and we move in it in a reactive state, we are lost. We are doomed to repeat the same mistakes in this life over and over as well as in the many lives to come. In order to get off of the *wheel of life* we must realize the truth and we must merge with God by whatever name. This can only be done through meditation, transformation of the ego, and then the destruction of the ego. That is the truth behind every resurrection story. If we want to be resurrected the false identity, the ego, has to die. When it dies we find life and resurrect the true self, which is one with Brahman.**

Teaching Us to Live in Maya
Chapter 9

Earlier in this book we discussed not only of the ego, but the censor. We only briefly mentioned the super-ego and the power that it has over us. **The super-ego is the internalization of all of the power-over voices with which we come in contact. It begins as the voice of the parents telling us what we should or shouldn't do. Later, in school, the teacher's voice begins to shape the superego. Eventually, through sheer repetition and the personality that we choose to form, we internalize the voice of the authority figure that tells us how we should behave in an unsure reality.**

It can affirm us as we do what we have been told, or criticize us when and if we don't. It can be a loving kind voice, but if it is negative, a harsh hurtful voice that is an evil task-master that never lets us feel good about ourselves. It can make demands constantly and then criticize us if we can't attain them; if it is hateful it will criticize us even if we do attain them by saying we didn't attain them well enough. There is no satisfying the superego, especially a negative one. Many psychologists work to strengthen the ego so that it can stand up against the onslaught of the superego and keep its boundaries strong enough to prevent a flood of its shadow side from rushing in to destroy the false identity that we created as self. **As we live in Maya we are conditioned to want to claim the false self as the only real self. We must fight off this temptation, or we will become trapped—ego bound, shutting off any access to Atman, that divine, eternal part of the self.**

If we look at Maya in the western sense, we can see a reflection of the ego that western civilization has created and strengthened for centuries. Freud's model of the mind was that we had the superego at the top as internalized, external voices of the parent or an authority figure working to keep the ego in line, so to speak. The ego was located in between the superego and the subconscious or the id. We talked about its function in the previous paragraph. The id was a dark, dangerous uncontrollable part of the mind that would destroy the ego if all of the repressed thoughts and images ever came rushing up into the conscious. Through psychoanalysis the ego was strengthened. Some of the shadow material in the id was slowly released and brought into the presence of the ego so that the libido, or the life energy that was used holding it down, could be released.

This strengthened the ego and helped facilitate both physical and mental health. When we look at western civilization and what I call the *Pyramid of History*, or the *Hierarchy of Worth* in a power-over society, we can see the same delineations. At the top of the pyramid we have an image of God that is actually similar to the superego.

The narrow view of God as understood in a power-over society is like a big, all powerful human being. This God loves his own and only his own. This God cannot abide sin and cannot abide lack of faith. He only draws close to those who have perfect faith and trust and are willing to do what he wants of them. If they do as he wants they become one of his group and they go to heaven after they die for an eternity. If they don't do as he demands, however, they are not only tortured by him, or by him turning his back on them and allowing just anything to happen to them in this world, their souls are also tormented forever.

I am not necessarily saying that this is the real God, or the one that I think of when I use the word, but this is the God of the institutional church. If we look at the Hebrew Scripture we can see where God's people were often told to destroy whole nations of people who were not part of his group because they were heathens who worshiped other Gods. If they didn't do this—override their own opinions of right and wrong and force themselves to be brutal, it was because they were faithless, bad, and condemned.

This example of God is an externalized, unhealthy superego. It is loving when we bend to its will, but brutal and hateful when we do not. It forces us to behave in ways that we do not like because it knows better than us, and is the ultimate good. The voices in the superego attack us sometimes, or manipulate us into carrying out the wishes of parents and society for the same reason: when we first internalized them the people who were giving us these rules were understood as being all loving and all knowing. Just as they weren't, in actuality, this God, the power-over God, isn't.

Those who accept this power-over God rationalize. They are scared to death to challenge these ideas. Their internal superego freezes them. They can't challenge this idea because it is their internal superego on steroids projected to the outside world. The answer for those who cannot withstand this idea of God is to rationalize that all that this God says is good. They try to move close to this God in the same way that abused children try to cling to an abusive parent in order to get at least some positive reinforcement. They fight to climb this pyramid like a ladder always looking up. Getting to the top means being like this God and behaving like this God.

This God is at the top of the pyramid, next comes human beings. The group of human beings that considers themselves most like this God also considers themselves to be better, and superior. As they do as this God is said to do: take care of their own and punish those who are weaker and who don't believe in this God, they gain power. Sometimes the identity of this God is even transposed and interchanged with other power-over, because the God is worshiped because it has power-over everything.

People who have power-over others through weapons and war, or by having a lot of money, which is a symbol of power in western society, consider themselves closer to God and more godly. The others who are lower on the pyramid support those near the top who are closer to God. Their objective is to climb up to the top of the pyramid by mimicking the group that is closer to God in thought and action.[8]

What happens because of this blindness and narrow view is that we end up with a pyramid or a ladder where several groups of people who identify with different races, ethnic groups, sexes and religions work with each other only so they can gain enough power to climb to the top of the pyramid toward God. Their group identities become solidified in this illusion of Maya as they push down others who they consider more inferior, because they are less powerful. Being less powerful means being less like God. Pushing the powerless down and lifting oneself toward godhood becomes a good thing in this scenario.

The next levels down on the pyramid are: the animals; the plants; and the earth. Each of these subcategories is divided into those that are superior and inferior. The species that have the most control over the other animals or can be used by human beings for their own purposes have more worth to the human family. If we just look at God, the Human Family, and lump the Animals, Plants and Earth together as soulless beings who are not like God, we coincidently come up with the same model as the one for the human mind—the superego, ego, and id. God is the superego, humanity is the ego, and animal, plants, and the earth are the id. By strengthening Humanity it becomes like God and some day will become God, according to many fundamentalist religions. The Human can also suppress the earth making it subordinate and using it for whatever the human family wants, just like the ego suppresses the id and uses its energy for what it wants when the ego gets healthy.

As a civilization in the west, and now in most of the world, we have internalized this external dominator system. Maya is now the identity and psyche of the human family. The group identity called humanity is the ego and the censor that doesn't allow us to break free. This identity is exemplified by the unshakable belief that the object of life is to move up that ladder toward God. As long as we believe this we cannot see the truth. As long as our identity and worth are based in Maya and in the pyramid we will be trapped and unable to think clearly; we will accept this world of Maya as the only important reality with everything outside of it secondary. When we can understand something on the outside and draw into Maya in order to buy or sell it our idea of Maya expands and the object becomes real and of value. This only assures that we stay trapped in Maya and our censor will never let us see this. The power of Maya, the power of the illusion keeps us locked in and our success in the illusion, our climbing the ladder, solidifies our false identity. We cannot see the truth because if we decide to take the next logical step it will mean death to the false identity.

If we will let go of our identity in the larger world and realize that the separation between the Pyramid and the outer reality is just an illusion, this realization will lead us on our first step to freedom from our false identity to our real identity as divine beings. It will cause a renaissance on earth. We cannot do this because of our corporate ego and the rules that we have set up to keep us from seeing the truth. Another word for this set of rules is *karma*. It is the very make up of the self that will not allow us to see all possibilities. There is individual karma and corporate karma. If one can break through one censor it is easier to break through the other, but the inner-censor working in unison with the outer one almost makes freedom impossible. The only valid path to freedom is dying. Freedom means dying to the individual identity and the corporate identity. When we have died we are resurrected as our true, spiritual selves. The Maya and our inner world, then begins to serve us instead of us constantly serving it out of blindness. We then become proactive instead of reactive, and we begin to serve the world as our *dharma*, or the *greater work* that makes the world better and introduces the Kingdom of Heaven into this reality by setting the blinded captives of the ego and the censor free.

The Pyramid of Success
Chapter 10

In order to be free of the world system we need to understand how we get sucked in so deeply. We can get sucked in by having our egos seduced when we are very young. Through inner thoughts and mental manipulation we can be shaped to take part in the deceptive system and to even think there is nothing else. We already spoke of classical conditioning and operant conditioning, when we discussed pairing what is considered *good* by society to certain behaviors and *bad* to certain behaviors in order to control our minds so we might suppress and internally oppress our own behaviors with no external intervention, but there are other ways that we are drawn in. The human mind has dynamic cognitive abilities that are so powerful that we can use our imaginations to shape our own behavior.

If we see a person behave a certain way and receive something good, we can imagine ourselves in that person's place and accept that the same behavior will bring us something good. If the person receives something bad, we can see them and realize that we will receive something bad, or we can even figure out how to change the behavior, slightly, and get something good. We become masters of our own fate, in our own minds, if nowhere else. We learn to create cause/response scenarios in our minds as we plot and plan in order to do certain behaviors that will bring about certain rewards.

Being good at creating such scenarios, if one does them well, helps one become a strong ego and climb the ladder of success. The ladder of success, in the western world, is very interesting. In the U.S., according to the propaganda, everyone has the opportunity to climb to the top. If one works hard there are no limits. It is as if we are all racing to climb to the top of the pyramid in order to receive fame, fortune, and the promise of freedom. When we enter the first stage of the pyramid there are a gate and gatekeepers. Before we are even allowed to compete we have to pass the *norms examiner*. We have to be close enough to the Good Normal to get into the door and even get a job.

The Good Normal person speaks like the people on TV. They are usually Caucasian and from fair to very attractive.

The more attractive, more middle class, and more Caucasian the job applicant, the better the likelihood of obtaining a job that will bring in a lot of money. The main requirement for many jobs is to be Caucasian and presentable, or at least like one. Now many people of color can enter the market, but when they do they at least have to be able to communicate like a Caucasian and have a good educational background. People of color usually end up being overqualified for jobs just to get in through the back door. And then the climb begins.

Usually the next step involves having the right education or paper trail. If one is educated and gets along with one's peers they usually move up the ladder to mid management. If one is a person of color it is more difficult. If many of one's peers are against it during the "water cooler" conversations people of color are passed over repeatedly. Sometimes one person of color makes it for the sake of appearance, but if there is one there is not likely to be two. As soon as the person of color makes it to mid-management they become representatives for their whole race and are loaded with the burden of helping support the people of their race below them, even though they really don't have any power themselves.

If one wants to go higher this usually occurs by networking. When the people higher discover a good worker who is willing to put in more time and energy than others and who cares more about the culture of the workplace than the culture of their race or gender, that person begins to climb the ladder. The more the person lets go of their individuality and ethnic culture and take on the corporate culture the higher he can climb, if he is competent. Much of the climbing, however, comes from who one knows more than what one knows.

With all people there is a ceiling they can't traverse. There are people, powers and principalities, that are in a totally different league above that ceiling and the only way to attain such power is to marry into it. Above that layer and governing everything is the *big lie*. It is the cornerstone of western Maya. The lie is that you are better than everyone below you in the hierarchy because you have power-over them; your value comes from that power and without it you are nothing like the many people below you on the pyramid.

The one that is willing to lose his soul the most will attain material goods. Others often end up in mid-management or all the way at the bottom. Some never make it into the back door. Success then, as defined by the societal paradigm, in reality, is nothing but a different type of slavery. Success is loss of the soul. It is solidifying the ego and surrounding oneself with a group of people that solidify the ego and make it impenetrable. It is the killing of the spirit. Though one may look healthy and famous after several years of this corrupting life, he eventually becomes spiritually dead. It is almost impossible for such a person to find redemption because he has created such a strong, tricky censor and ego that he will convert any message that would free him into a threatening, evil proposition.

Success in the world of men means death in the spirit, unless one becomes enlightened first. When one has

transformed the ego, transcended the emptiness of the need to possess many worldly goods, and then ultimately transcends the ego one enters into life. This can't be done without finding a good, spiritual teacher or a real spirituality, and breaking the bands of Maya. When one breaks free from Maya, one has life. It is difficult to do so. There are no new models for doing so, but there are many old ones.

The alchemists used to say that one found the gold by searching through the dung. One could find the best thing, the thing that would heal the system, by looking at what was thrown out. In western civilization spirituality was thrown out. Love, kindness, patience and union with God were thrown out in favor of empire building, making money, and going to a respectable church to be a respectable, religious person. The "fire insurance" religions took the place of real spirituality and hardened the individual and societal ego even more. As a result of this abdication of their religious and prophetic charge to keep the society healthy and to lead the society forward so that every individual would become a greater person, the world began to fall apart and still is.

From this religious bankruptcy came just about every type of dysfunction: global warming; an increase in teen pregnancy; an increase in violence; religious wars; church scandals because of sexual improprieties; and many other problems that come from living in an ego based society instead of a God, i.e., love based society. This was all based on the precepts of a power-over church that supported war, violence, segregation, and a power-over God figure that didn't resemble the God of love taught by many great teachers and mystics. **The only way out of all of the problems in the world today is the dissolution of the ego. The ego must die. The energy used to support the false identity must be used to resurrect each individual and to resurrect the world.**

The ego was a good idea. It helped each of us learn how to make it through the world as young children and taught us how to survive, but it soon became like the runaway corporation implanted into our psyches. We are now supporting it instead of it supporting us. We support it with our livelihood while it keeps us alive by giving us just enough crumbs to live as zombies obeying its every wish. It is time for us to overthrow the ego and all of the negative messages and ideas that serve as the censor so we can be the free, divine individuals we would like.

When we overthrow the ego we need not worry about racism, sexism, homophobia, domestic violence, robbery, theft, or the many problems that plague human society any longer. When we get rid of the ego we will become our divine selves and we will have enough of everything including self-worth and love. The world is ours. There is enough food and shelter for everyone, but we can't see this. The ego always wants more. Everything isn't enough for the ego. The ego lives in fear, anger, and greed. It wants and wants, sometimes only so others can't have, because it is afraid of scarcity and real competition.

We are slaves to the ego. We perform like domesticated animals because the ego is domesticated and we think that we are the ego. It is time for us to let go of the ego by seeking reality whole-heartedly and making sure that we find it. The ego fears death....especially its own. It will do anything to keep us from finding the true light, including providing us with false lights. The source of these false lights is the externalized world that resembles the human mind enough to deceive us. In actuality, however, we have created the *memes* (social genetic code) of the external society too.

External religion is empty. It consists of following several rules and rituals that we usually don't understand. What is considered mystical and being close to God in such religions is often not the real thing. The false mysticism pushed by such institutions often has nothing to do with divine union. Those who claim to be spokes-persons for God and who claim to be connected with God in these instances are often worse than people who don't even go to places of worship. The religions are failing us miserably. Our religious leaders don't know what they are doing unless they are ego free and connected with God. Unfortunately, many aren't. We have substituted diplomas and degrees for a relationship with God in many instances when we consider ministers. Those without a great deal of money, time, and intelligence can't even afford to attend seminaries most of the time. If God calls a poor person to be a minister how does that work? There is something wrong

The only way to break this downward spiral is to break free from the ego and the ides in the larger society that support it. It is time for us to die.

To Obtain Enlightenment
Section 4

Death by Love
Chapter 11

There are many opportunities to die, spiritually, if one is truly willing. As I speak of dying spiritually I am not speaking about dying of boredom as in some of our religious institutions, I am talking about the death of the ego. In just about every religion there is a story of death and resurrection. This is nothing to just read about it. Reading about someone else's death and resurrection and identifying with it doesn't mean that we have gone through the process, though many religions would have us believe so. One must take her own cross and follow the one who was crucified and resurrected.

The spiritual path is very difficult. It takes one to very ugly places. It drags one all the way down into the subconscious to face their negative ego and negative superego. These are the places within the psyche from whence come all of the horrible beliefs, values, and self hatred. Everything that has been done to us resides in the subconscious. Some of the things that hurt us so badly that we can't even speak of them are right down there alive and well, affecting what we do in our lives. In order to be free,

one has to face nightmare like creatures knowing that they will feel as alive now as they did when they really happened.

To deal with this *journey to the underworld*, as they called it in various religions, there used to be gods and goddesses that would accompany us there. They were represented by dark, dangerous, powerful archetypes. In western civilization most of them were demonized. They were associated with darkness, which became associated with evil. All of the loving gods and goddesses that would accompany us became demons and the primary response to them was to avoid them. The primary response to depression, pain, or anger, was to get away from it as quickly as possible, anyway possible even if it meant taking drugs that would destroy one's liver and digestive system..

When people have the dark-night-of- the-soul experience now, they are given *Prozac.* Depression is understood as an illness. The symptom is treated, but never the inner cause. If we ever took the time to look at the cause of it, however, we would see that the cause is the artificial lives we are forced to live in the power-over pyramid. One needs to have a very hard heart to live in a world of plenty with people starving close by, or with people dying because they can't afford health care.

We see so many ugly things day after day, and the person who is considered healthy psychologically, learns to block them out. He learns to harden his heart and not think of it. While he is blocking out the emotions of love and compassion, however, and just trying to save them for his close friends and family, his capacity to feel them even for them diminishes. He no longer feels real love, but an imitation without the fire of compassion. He can treat his children horribly, his spouse, and his friends, and still say that he loves them because he doesn't really know what love is anymore.

He can go to church and pray—say he loves God and his neighbor, and then break all of the ideals of God and treat his neighbor horribly. He can quote scripture one Sunday and call himself Pro-Life, and in the next breath he can support cutting social services, increasing soldiers and war funding, and throwing unwed mothers off of public assistance. To anyone on the outside this seems unnatural and immoral, but not to him. He has split himself in half. He can't see the hypocrisy of the situation. He doesn't know what love is because he doesn't know how to feel. Why can't he feel(?), because he is ego-bound.

His ego does whatever it can to protect itself. His censor blinds him so he cannot see the hypocrisy, because he would have to change if he saw it. He is living in a world of dualism where everything is right or wrong. If he saw what was happening and didn't do anything he would be considered bad, so he refuses to see it. In truth this dichotomy doesn't exist. When one is free of the ego one just is. One is not good or bad.

When one loses the need to be right, wrong, good, bad, and becomes a real person one stays in the center of reality. Two opposing ideas or situations can occur within the self and she can sit with them in the midst of the fire of paradox. She can live in the midst of the paradox and draw energy from the tension that will lead her to truth. Her first action is not to get away from discomfort or darkness, it is to explore it to find the meaning. Only by descending into the underworld and overcoming it can we find our true, divine selves. In order to be a free person one needs to enter into the darkness or emptiness.

The Dark God or Goddess that accompanies us through this journey is none other than Atman. The Atman is that spark of God that dwells within. It is the divine self. It is our true self that is locked up within the ego and surrounded by the censor. When we descend into the underworld and the ego splits, or is burned up and the censor is cast into the fire, the released power allows the Atman to move us from the dark, fearful subconscious up into the light. We become our divine selves as we release all of the energy that has been bottled up below and bring it into the conscious to be burned off through contemplation and meditation. **This occurs because of the power of Atman within, and the power of Brahman, or God in the universe that draws us upward to a higher vibration.**

When we reunite with Brahman, our true selves, we become co-creators in the world. There is a real born again experience that is more than *name it and claim it*. In reality we remember who we are and what this world is. **When we have remembered, the world has no power over us. We are in the world, but not of the world, and the world is within us, because we are all things.**

One need not wait until he or she dies to experience heaven; one can experience it now. The Kingdom of Heaven is not out there somewhere it is within each of us. The object of this life is to enter into that Kingdom and live in it on Earth as it is in Heaven. When we have done that, remembered who we really are, we will have attained true freedom—eternal freedom. This may seem like the end of the journey, but in reality, it will have just begun. When we are free of the ego, we become magical beings who can live as we want. This was the goal of the soul that was birthed into this world. The ego was the training wheels for the beginning journey, now it is time to remove them. The survival of the Earth and humanity may depend on it.

Fourth Order Thinking
Chapter 12

Up to about fifty years ago the world was easy to understand. Every one lived in their isolated, little cultures creating stories about the way of the world and their ancestors' greatness. We all learned about values. We knew what was right and wrong—we learned it from the churches, public schools, newspapers, radio, and television. Our scientists performed experiments so they could understand more about our world and the universe, and passed their truth onto us as a mother bird gives food to its child. We were moving *onward and upward forever*, as everyone was saying, but then something happened: The

Sixties Revolution, Television and the Internet—especially the Internet.

The Internet was the pinnacle of an inward revolution that began in the sixties in the United States. A more educated youth evolved as they partook of the new tool called Television, for the first time, began to see the world outside of their own small communities. People had been raised in communities segregated by race and class. Prejudices had been fed to them from birth.

Along with concern and truth each child was served up prejudice, hatred and some type of *ism* and weaned on it. Radio, teachers, clergy and well meaning adults helped support the lies. An anti-racism trainer once referred to the process as *poison in the cookies.* As long as they were kept separate from the other they accepted these lies. The culture had to form a group mind. What better way in a very authoritarian, but democratic society to keep a person engaged in the group agenda than to make them fear anyone outside and feel superior. This was happening in just about every community in the U.S.

And then something horrible happened, desegregation. People began to meet each other. They discovered that the people they had learned to hate and fear were not very different. They discovered that their loving parents, teachers, ministers and leaders had been lying to them and using them for their own ends. The people in the suburbs and inner cities began to realize that they were being used, and there was an explosion of activity. Much of it was focused around women's rights, civil rights, and the peace movement. The news media, especially on Television, aired what was really happening during the Vietnam War, civil rights marches, and women's rights marches. Many of the dispossessed groups began to join together and to work together as a result of this. When the common people saw the ugliness perpetrated by a system that claimed to believe in liberty and justice for all they were outraged. Many began to identity with people being oppressed and things began to change.

After the sixties the human rights marches began to lose energy. The anti-war movement grew in power, because it was visible everywhere and very powerful, but after the end of the Vietnam War there seemed to be silence. The agents of change for our nation that were pushing for human rights weren't covered as much anymore by the news media, to any extent, so they seemed to have disappeared. Eventually the media was sold to six corporations whose interest was to preserve the status quo. Thus came the end of the reporting of social activism, until the Internet

One computer scientist created the back-bone for a system that could connect computers all over the world. Anyone could sit home on their personal computer and communicate with people all over the world. He patented the Internet, but left it available to the public. His generosity and intelligence changed the world. This was a revolution of knowledge that would bring in a new age of reason.

The media was no longer needed. Anyone could communicate on the Internet. They could put up websites, they could broadcast, and they could provide alternative news. Now people can even upload videos and pictures on the Internet for everyone in the world to see. There is information exchange everywhere so the lies, the poison in the cookies, about various ethnic groups, races, genders and people with different sexual orientations are much harder to swallow. The fearful leaders who kept the public locked in fear have lost a lot of their power. Any thinking individual can now go to the Internet and check the facts to see if they are true. This is being done everyday.

One major thing that has come from the Internet is a deep exploration of many cultures around the world. Before being exposed to such cultures we believed that our way was the right way. The United States and western countries struggled to export their culture everywhere because they considered it the best and the only way that worked. Through the Internet we found that almost every culture worked. We discovered that people could live in ways that were opposite to our own and that they worked. People could be just as healthy, happy and educated as us and live a totally different way. This discovery began to destroy the idea of western superiority. More than that, it created a curiosity in the younger generations that can't be snuffed. The younger generation is not willing to live by the old, suffocating power-over rules. We don't know what to expect from them.

All of the new interaction and ideas have caused problems for those who want to be in charge and who want to co-opt the power and energy of the public to support their idea of what the world should be. We know that there can be more than one way of living. We realized that there can be more than one truth. We realized that there can be several correct ways of doing things and they can be the opposite. We are meeting people from various cultures daily on the Internet and in our own neighborhoods. In order for the world to survive and for us to survive as a people, we must internalize the fact that the world is not easy to understand. There is no one way. No one group of people is better than the other. A global society is being forced upon us and if we don't adapt to it and allow our minds and our understanding about the world to expand we may destroy ourselves as a species.

Our technology has given us the power to destroy on a major scale. With all of the fighter jets, cruise missiles, and nuclear warheads we could actually destroy the whole world for the first time in history, or make it so miserable that no one would want to live on it. Pollution, Global Warming, destruction of the ozone layer, and the extinction of thousands of species everyday are a problem that on one nation can address. All nations must work together to address these issues. Mega tribalism, or Nations, must be done away with and we must understand that we are humans first and then whatever designations we make. It would be better to realize that we are divine beings, but I don't know that some people will ever make it that far.

As long as we are trapped in our egos and lower forms of thinking there is a chance for extinction of all life on earth. We must develop what is known as *Fourth Order Thinking*. I would like to explain Fourth Order Thinking by comparing it to the other orders of thought.

First Order Thinking is very conflictual. When someone disagrees with the First Order thinker the response from the First Order thinker is: You have to go because you are in my way. When someone disagrees with the **Second Order thinker** the response is similar, but not as psychotic. It would be: You make me sick. The **Third Order thinker** is somewhat more sophisticated. Most of the intelligent people in the world are at this level. The Third Order thinker would respond: I am feeling sick when you say that. In this scenario the listener is taking at least some responsibility for the way they are feeling. **The Fourth Order thinker** would go deeper and would facilitate better communication. A Fourth Order Statement: When I heard things like you are saying in the past they always resulted in someone getting hurt so what you are saying doesn't feel good to me. Can you explain it?

As you may notice, the First Order person is little more than psychotic. Many people in the world don't think like this, but there are still people who are in power-over positions who are quite sociopathic, who feel this way about competitors or employees they consider disloyal. Second Order people are somewhat immature and not ready to take responsibility for their own feelings. They are only responding to the outside world reactively instead of proactively. Someone is always responsible for doing something to them. Third Order the person is trying to own his or her own feelings realizing that something inside him or her is being sparked by what the other person is saying. This is a very mature person. The Fourth Order person has gone further. He or she knows what is being touched by the person and is communicating that to the person and trying to see if their response is called for in reality, or if they are hearing something wrongly. It is an attempt to clarify the situation through open dialog instead of closing down the conversation by posturing.

This is the type of thinking needed in diverse community where conversation is difficult and there are often misunderstandings. This would mean, however, that the two people engaged would be mature enough to consider they may be making a mistake or hearing each other the wrong way. A person with a weak psyche, or lost in the zombie box of the ego can never do this. This, however, must happen if the world is to survive. **Since the arrested ego has the impediment, the best way to make this happen is to get rid of the ego. It is necessary to do the inner-work to transform the ego and then to transcend the ego. This is the only hope for humanity. The ego is full of all kinds of false ideas and extreme rules that may have worked for an infant who needed to learn how the world in which he was born worked, but they don't work anymore.** During frustrating circumstances the ego spills them out automatically. It recreates the stress and tension that comes with the false idea that one way is the right way wherever we go. We end up destroying the peace that we want because of the ego.

We look for peace and wholeness, but our ego driven desire to compete and come out on top sabotages it. War violence, racism, sexism, all of the isms come from the ego trying to create and recreate the world as we experienced it as children. The ego has to go; it, along with the superego, has to die and the easy dualist answers have to be tossed into the toilet. We need to do the inner-work to cleanse our minds and hearts, and then we can be guided by them. As long as the ego and the censor are in charge, however, controlling us and moving us to live out our fantasies this will not happen. We will be lost.

Shaolin priests once said that we spend too much time working outside of ourselves. They say that we are constantly shining the light of awareness into the outer world. We are putting our time and energy into the outer world trying to create a safe, secure place for ourselves and our loved ones. As we use our energies and awareness outside, however, only darkness and ignorance grow and dwells within. We become hopeless; our lives become miserable and we become angry and reactive instead of proactive. When we turn the light of awareness inside, however, and work at healing and strengthening the inside, we automatically conquer that which is outside. We embody what we want our external world to be and from that place, a foundation of self love and being, we create our desired path daily.

We have learned to live the wrong way. We use most of our energy working on the outside and then we use a little bit of time each day to work inside. We should be using most of our time and energy to work inside and then using the leftover time to work outside. If we did this we could easily reconnect with God and become vessels filled with the light of truth and the creative power of the divine. How can we do this? By becoming spiritual warriors and destroying all of the inner lies, deceptions, maladaptive ideas, and eventually the ego itself with the sword of truth.

On Being the Warrior
Chapter 13

The Warrior archetype has been changed. When we think of the warrior we often think of the soldier. The soldier is someone who lays down his life for his country, but the soldier is also one who firstly obeys orders.[9] In the best of circumstances soldiers will use their better judgment if they are ordered to do something inhumane. There are crimes against humanity. The soldier should refuse to follow orders that would result in those crimes. In reality soldiers who do this are often court-marshaled. If they cannot be punished legally in public they are usually chastised behind the scene. Many are passed over for promotions, given the worse jobs possible and sometimes, as in the case of the Marines where one has to receive promotions to stay in, they are forced out. Most soldiers, therefore, will not challenge their superiors.

The Warrior, however, is a person dedicated to a certain code. The Warriors in Native American societies did not follow orders, they worked together to create the orders. They were all clear thinking leaders who were in great mental, physical, and spiritual shape. The first objective of the Warrior was to destroy the part of herself that was causing most of the damage. The anger, greed, fear, hatred and many such emotions, and the wrong thought patterns had to be destroyed. Secondly the warrior destroyed anything that threatened to destroy his community including lies and false ideals. It is time for us to reclaim the warrior archetype. Until we can there will be no peace and no society where there is love and justice.

The inner-work, the work of creating health, prosperity, peace and love inside, begins with renewing the mind and the thoughts and ideas that have been planted in us. **Shunyamurti Robert Shubow describes seven steps to accomplishing true warrior-hood and the enlightenment that follows. The first step and most important is removing the B.R.A.I.N S.L.U.D.G.E.**

Brain Sludge is an acronym for many of the maladaptive thoughts, ideas and tendencies that influence the ego and thus our thoughts and behaviors. Below you will find a brief definition of each one. In previous chapters we have discussed many.

B—Binarism (binary, dualistic thinking)

R—Reification (thingifying). The universe is a community of subjects, but in our society we make everything into objects that are apart from ourselves.

A—Adaptation. We must fight the desire to adapt to systems that are maladaptive and going in the wrong direction. This involves giving up the need to feel good about ourselves by receiving outside approval and being judged by or judging ourselves by external standards created for us.

I—Identification (any personal identification) It means letting go of the roles we have been assigned including religion, race, sex, sexual orientation—any roles, so we can become our true, pristine self.

N—Nihilism. (hopelessness and negativity) Nihilism is self defeating and useless. It destroys any opportunity for freedom and gratitude, never allowing us to see the possibilities that present themselves before is in the world and in the universe. The lack of energy that comes as a result of it strengthens the ego and locks us into the world of illusion.

S—Superficiality (a shallow society). We live in a shallow society where deep thinking and the ability for profound thought is not fostered. We learn to think on the surface so we never enter the true depths of reality.

L—Longings (dissatisfaction). People are often dissatisfied with what they have in western society. Satisfaction is seen as an impediment to growth and success. Satisfaction and the desire to improve and get more are seen

110

as opposites in our society, so we are always longing for what we don't have and ignoring that which we have.

U—Undermining. The undermining of each other in a competitive society in order to reach higher ground, have more power and feel superior.

D—Domination (one-up-manship). The need to always be better than the other and to be in control.

E—Externalization (projection). Projecting one's own ego fantasies onto the world and other people when they often have nothing to do with others.

We can remove the brain sludge by working with the right spiritual director and through meditation and contemplation. Meditation burns away all of this Brain Sludge, by bringing us face to face with the divine. This closeness to the divine power and our inner divine self, Atman, begins to burn away old thought patterns. Our minds are like cups of muddy water. As we sit quietly without internal words our mind begins to settle. The maladaptive thoughts and idea settle down and leave a mind that is like a clear smooth pond. In that pond we possess the reflection of the moon.

The Atman, the divine spark within, is a reflection of the heavenly divine spark. The Atman is like the moon reflecting the divine energy of the sun and moving the tides. As we develop the Atman, setting it free from its imprisonment in the ego and the censor, the Atman, like the moon floating on a pond, begins to float on top of the psyche as the dominate self. If the pond is disturbed is the reflection of the moon disturbed? No, it isn't, because the moon is free from any of the effects of the pond. Even so, as we develop our Atman, or true self, we find that we are independent of external and internal circumstances. The path to freedom is the transformation and then eradication of the ego. This all begins with sitting and with working to clear the brain sludge.

Through Atman Analysis sessions and spiritual guidance we can explore the subconscious through our deep rooted dreams. Many of these dreams are communications from the Atman, the divine self, as it works around the censor to pass on the messages we need in this lifetime to obtain enlightenment. Others may be our fears and worries being expressed by the ego or super ego, but even these can give insights on what is happening inside. All of these dreams can be considered downloads of information from the ultimate, divine conscious. If we can understand them, or be given clear understanding by a spiritual guide an open dialog between the divine consciousness and the ego self begins. We are ultimately freed from our illusion as we heal the split off parts of ourselves and then transcend the ego altogether.

The second step in our deep inner work is to abandon the fantasies that underlie the ego identity. We have all learned who we are, what we are supposed to be and how we compare to others. We have discussed how so many of these early ideas shape our identities and personalities. They

112

create an underlying matrix in our minds. Everything that we see and understand is only understood through this matrix. The matrix is somewhat like a stencil. It blocks out things that threaten our false identity, lets those in that supports it, and can even change those things that would change it into things that support it.

This can be seen with many of the religions. Many of them are started by a mystic who has a direct interaction with the Divine. This person brings this new found truth to the world. Some people are happy to hear it. They become free and enlightened. As time passes, however, those who follow begin to change the religion. Eventually the religion that was universal and meant to free us from our false idea of separateness begins to promote the idea of a special chosen people. Instead of healing the separateness it begins to set up a new hierarchy of separateness. As time goes it gets worse until it is part of the system that promotes power-over. The system is then worse off than it was before.

Just as the religion becomes part of the matrix in the external world, in the hierarchy of oppression, it also becomes part of the internal matrix. Thoughts and ideas that were meant to free us feed the ego. We begin to think that we are more truthful, more loving, and more enlightened than those outside of our belief system. As a result of this we become less loving, less kind, unenlightened, and angry. This, of course, is disguised under the rhetoric of our new found belief system. Our ego clings to the rhetoric and the censor works to reinforce the desire of the ego to immerse itself in it. In the gospels this process is described by Jesus as a demon being cast out of a person. It goes around looking for a new place. When it comes back it finds its old place all beautiful and decorated it goes back and finds seven worse than itself and moves back in. At the end of this parable is said, "So it is with this wicked generation."

As it is with our system, so it is with each individual within the system. The matrix, therefore, the whole thing, must be done away with. By the age of five we are given a matrix that we are working to support or fight against until we die. This is not necessary. We can do away with this by getting pass our ego identity and becoming our self-actualized, divine selves. It takes our will, our desire, and then the necessary work to do so.

Step three consists of letting go of the belief systems that support our insanity and blindness. It means letting go of all belief systems and formulas. All of them are tainted. All of them that are created within the dominator/oppressor system work to bring about dualism and dominator/oppressor mentality within us. We must let go of the belief systems and the false identities and go straight to the source to attain truth. We must learn to connect with and trust the deeper knowledge that comes from within. When we let go and reach a state called nirvikalpa Samadhi (residing in the place beyond thought constructs) the creative union that takes place within spreads itself through us taking the place of external belief systems. This is the true union with God. Through the practice of savikalpa Samadhi, or stilling the thoughts in the mind, we attain nirvikalpa Samadhi, which is residing in a place beyond the thought constructs and distortions of the mind.

This level can be reached by attaining Madhya, or the midpoint between the out-breath and in-breath, or thought. In between the breaths thought stops and there is silence. Through meditative practices we can learn to expand that silence. As we expand the silence in the mind that takes place between the breaths we ultimately move beyond the words. We lose faith in the words realizing that the words are simply a sign for concepts and ideas and not objects and ideas. A sign is something that points to something else. It gives us a direction in which to proceed. A symbol does not point to something else; it is the representation of something else that exists in nature. People often think of language as a symbol, in truth, however, it is a sign. It is necessary for us to realize the different between symbols and signs and to realize that language does not represent a substantial thing out there.

Symbols are only available to us when we get beyond language. When we are free of all of the verbiage during meditation we find the only true symbols that exist within the self and in the subconscious, or they will present themselves to us through dreams administered by our divine Atman self.

The fourth step suggested by Shunyamurti Robert Shubow, is achieving a state of dynamic equilibrium within

our psyches. We must put away all of the dualistic ideas that hold us hostage by examining them deeply and challenging there veracity. We must pull together things that the system has separated as opposites like science and the arts, or science and religion. We must find a balance between being and doing, and between being and the act of becoming.

Doing can look very much like being. One can perform tasks with grace and agility by doing. When one looks at a very technical basketball player, one can see the way he moves and the way that he scores. He can see how crisp his passes are and how tight his defense is as he keeps the opposing player out of the optimal shooting area. The technical basketball player scores high and well. He is a good player who scores consistently and is an asset to the team. In comparison there is the basketball player who works from a place of being. This type of basketball player would be considered a great basketball player like Charles Barkley, who does everything well on the court. He seems to flow around his opponents like water as he moves the ball.

He, the ball, and the sport have become one. He is always in the zone, because he is not acting the part of the basketball player, he is being the basketball player and the game and the basketball. There is a spiritual element to his playing. He is connected to everything and downloading his talent, skills, and movements. This is the difference between being and doing.

There were many mathematicians in the world during the time of Albert Einstein, yet he stands out. There were many musicians during the time of Mozart, yet he stands out. These men and men like them stand out because they some how crossed the bridge from doing, and maybe even doing very well, to being the art they practiced. We can all do this also, but in a greater sense; life and everything in it can be our art as we download the infinite power and knowledge of the divine source into our lives.

As we live in a state of being, creating and moving through this great dream that we call reality, we realize that we are also becoming. We are deceived into thinking that we are living in two realities—one on the phenomenal, earthly plane and one on the nominal plane. We think that we are becoming something greater on the phenomenal plane while we have become our true selves on the nominal plane. In truth, however, there is no difference. We have already become the source of all things. We have become the dreamer of this dream called life and are living in a state of being and bliss. This awareness is something that must be realized as we live in a state of being. The state of being is a state of balance in all areas of our lives.

In relationships we need to have a balance between love and the law. There must be a balance between joy and gravity, and we must understand the difference between being in the world and the world being in us. This dynamic equilibrium comes when we let go of all of the polar, dualistic ideas and stop accepting them as real. As we live in the place of paradox and dynamic tension we begin to experience real life. We begin to know the correct times and

seasons for each action. Life becomes like jazz and we live in the flow state, instead of moving together lock step in a linear fashion.

When we create lives that are not based on the false assumption of dualism and live lives based on the fact that things are always moving and changing and not standing still, we have true lives. We become dynamic beings who replicate the dynamic movement and dance of the universe. If we are to be free dualism must be put to death and we must live each and every day at the center of reality. As the Shaolin say, "We must stand in the door of reality without flinching." When we can do that, we will be energetic, dynamic and co-creators with God. We can recreate this balance and move to flow state permanently, but in order to do so we must apply the creative tools that every human being has been supplied: Faith; Love; Openness; and Will Power.

We must have faith in ourselves and God. We must believe that it is possible to overcome the powers of the system and our ego before we start. Without faith we will not take the first step and nothing will happen. We all have a measure of faith. Every time any one of us pulls out a chair and sits we believe that chair will hold us. There have been times when chairs have collapsed underneath people. We sit down, however, because we don't believe that it will in our case, but it could. The same is true when we take on a spiritual path. When we have faith we move with certainty. We look forward to the results with hope, partially knowing what is going to happen.

When we sit in that chair we know what will happen. We don't know what will happen while we are in the chair. We don't know exactly how it will feel under us, but we know that it will hold us up. When we take on a spiritual path, striving for a particular goal we don't know exactly what it will look like. It could even be a disappointment. It could possibly collapse under us, but deep in our hearts we know that it will not. It is an understanding that goes far beyond rationalism. It is a knowledge that comes from the heart. In order to sincerely break free from the false dream that we call reality we need to be able to follow our heart knowledge and use this faith to reach more truthful planes of reality.

We also need love. We need the unconditional love spoken of as Agape. This is a love that gives without expectation of receiving back. It is unconditional and non-attached to outcome. As we love and fill ourselves with the power of love we become empty vessels filled with the embodiment of love that many call God. Love is the most powerful force in the universe and the nature of the universe, as experienced by those who have moved beyond the ego, is joy and love.

As we are filled with joy and love we reconnect ourselves with God and the reality that lies behind the false ideas that create the ego and keep our divine self, Atman, bound up behind the bars of fear and anger.

It is said that perfect love casts out all fear. When we begin to walk in love and contain the love within us there is no room for fear and anger. We become living, breathing extensions of the universe and God. This is our true identity. As we identify as beings of love and live our love and truth we reunite with the divine and become channels for this unconditional love on earth. We become what Meister Eckhart described as "mothers of God birthing God into existence through our acts and our very being."

When we can love unconditionally and trust God to lead us on the right path, we can be open without fear. We need not close ourselves off from our experiences. We need not check every experience and idea against the ideas given us by various religions or philosophies before we accept them, we can trust our hearts. We can be open to new thoughts and ideas and we can filter them through the eyes of love.

If we are open, yet discerning, we will continue to grow in power, grace, and wisdom. We will grow as we remove old ways of thinking and false belief systems, peeling them away like the layers of an onion until we arrive at emptiness. In that emptiness we will find all of eternity. We will find the creative power that is constantly creating and recreating the world.

This emptiness is celebrated in many forms. It is the dance of Shiva. The very name Yahweh is translated as the verb of being and also as that which creates. That dynamic power that created the universe is what can be found at the core of every human being, but in order to find it we must be willing to seek. As we hear new ideas, discover new paths, and learn more of the mundane truth we become more capable of experiencing the absolute truth. Absolute truth cannot be discussed, only experienced. Other truths and ideas, however, that can lead us to absolute truth, have been encoded in various myths, religions, stories, and even in the images in our dreams. If we can begin to understand these truths they will lead us to absolute truth. If we are not open, however, we will be frozen and stagnate as we read about other people's experiences with God but never have them. If we want to have these experiences we must focus our energies and actively seek understanding of the mundane truths and the experiences of actual truth. We do this by using our will power.

We set our mind on our goal and we work to attain it. We work in the middle of opposites as we struggle and strive to arrive at truth while at the same time relaxing and receiving what comes with joy. We work hard, yet we relax. We are serious, yet we are joyful. We are living in the paradox. In this paradox between opposites we are living in a state of dynamic balance using the energy of the pull of the two opposites to stop the entropy, the state of decay that often happens in systems over time, and to change this decay into what is known as life. For it is the dynamic energy of life that halts entropy and gives the human being the power to fly by rising up to a higher level of wisdom and understanding. This higher wisdom and understanding is known as love. It is living in the flow, living a life of jazz, and being one with the ultimate source of love called God.

This state of balance is very important. The first step to attain it is to let go of all ideals, let go of all identifications, and to slay the demon named dualism. When dualism is gone we move to step five: we acquire the mahavidia—the great understanding of reality. When we attain it we begin to share it through what is known as karma yoga. Karma yoga is a work that is done in order to free souls and uplift the whole of creation. Karma yoga and its outcome can be compared to the greater-work of transformation in which every individual should be taking part.

We human beings have the gift and the creativity to either work to enhance creation and all of its creatures or destroy it. The average human being contributes to the destruction of the planet through her lifestyle in a power-over society. The hierarchical thinking promotes degradation of the environment as well as lack of respect and care for those who are higher and lower than us in the pecking order. Most of the care that we show for others is to gain some type of self esteem.

I have heard many people say that they would like to help people who are more unfortunate because they feel good when they do that. Some have many things and feel that it is their obligation to help those who are unfortunate. The question is, are they helping the unfortunate for the sake of the unfortunate or to relieve their own guilt? How many times have you seen people working to help one group or the other and then ending up protecting them and treating them as though they are their children? When the children want to grow up and take responsibility for themselves or their own community there is usually a blow up and a feeling of betrayal by such helpers. The person who has given all of his or her time and energy feels betrayed. After all the work they have done the group suddenly wants to take over and do their own work. That is supposed to be the objective when working with people. The objective is not to own a select group of people like pets or like a pet project, so to speak, it is to educate them, strengthen them, and eventually develop a relationship with them as peers, not someone who is being served. Those who are ego bound and bound by the externalized ego that we call society, however, cannot see this, so the thing they would call good is bad.

When they depend on helping others to feel good about themselves and all their life is built around helping others what do they do when there is no one to help? It is important to help oneself first and come to a place of security, mental health, and awareness. One must strip away one's own ego before one can help other people break free from the chains of a dominator society. This is why the inner-work is important. After the inner-work one moves to the outer-work and the greater- work. The outer-work is what we talked about in previous chapters. The outer-work is showing a group of people what power they have and teaching them by example and by word, to be free; even free from the teacher—in other words, even free from us.

When one is being guided by love and is a vessel of love, one considers working with others dharma. It is an act

of God being done through us. We do it with no attachment to outcome and with no desire for glory. We sacrifice our pride into the fire of love. We put our egos into the fire of love and allow our works, our thoughts and our minds to be purified by the power of God. This makes any type of work, whether it is fighting for social justice, charity, or whatever, into karmic yoga. The difference between karmic yoga and doing good is that one just perpetuates the system and reinforces our power-over identification, while the latter destroys the false designation and recognizes that we human beings are all one and the artificial system of rewards and punishments is just that—artificial. We are like a society of individuals put in distant corners by a frustrated first grade teacher with our noses pressed against the wall because we were too curious, playful, or lively. It is time for us to turn around and notice that the room is full of people, and that they are all standing in corners. All it takes to connect is a few steps, the extension of the hand, or just showing that we care by saying, "You aren't alone. I'm here too and we can help each other. First let's just leave these corners and sit down together in the middle of the room."

What we offer as we lead people to empowerment and enlightenment is the only type of freedom that exists in the world. In step five we begin to help others while purifying ourselves. We purify ourselves until we even surpass the need to do karmic yoga anymore and move to six. In six we become the radiance of the hidden treasure, or the kingdom of God that we have found in our heart. We become the light of the world and begin to draw those who seek the light.

Our works and acts come from the very core of our being as our divine selves begin to live in, move in, and breathe in us as we usher the beauty, grace, love, and power of God into the world. When we do this, we become free and we begin to free the world. At this stage the ego, which has been transformed, begins to dissolve. We blend with, and begin to live in union with the divine accepting the fact that there is only One.

Conclusion

Step seven leads us to the realization that we are one with God and that we human beings are all one in the Kingdom of Heaven. When I say that we are one with God I mean that we are really *one with God.* This is not metaphorical or allegorical. We are one with Brahman. We are the ones who dream this reality into being like the Brahman, according to Hindu teachings, dreams the universe into being. We are both the dreamer (Brahman) and the dream. We are the vessels that give the dreamer the opportunity to manifest him or herself into the dream. Our sacrificed ego has led us to life and given us the power to recreate the world. As we recreate the world, as we re-dream the world, the old painful world around us begins to dissolve and we create the Kingdom of Heaven, or Sat Yuga, wherever we go.

The very fabric of the universe—this Earthy plane, is changed. A new reality breaks forth—one that we and like-minded individuals create through our lives as *divine beings.* When we are through with these seven steps, we can change the

126

world and break free from the brainwashing. This is the last step. Nothing else is needed, nor shall it ever be in the life to come or for all eternity once we take this step, because we are completely free of all Karma and able to stay on the wheel of life or remove ourselves from it any time we would like.

.

Notes

1. *Making Birth Safe in the U. S.,*
http://hospitalbirthdebate.blogspot.com/2006/12/how-long-does-it-take-memory-to-fade.html, Pre and Prenatal Psychology PhD and MA programs http://www.sbgi.edu/html/ppn1.html, www.trauma-pages.org

Perry (1997a), Incubated in Terror, Neurodevelopmental Factors in the Cycle of Violence
Citation: Perry, BD (1997). Incubated in Terror:
Neurodevelopmental Factors in the 'Cycle of Violence' In: Children, Youth and Violence: The Search for Solutions (J Osofsky, Ed.). Guilford Press, New York, pp 124-148.

2. Psychoanalytic Electronic Publishing, http://www.pep-web.org/document.php?id=ijp.073.0179a
 Volkmar, F.R. (1992). The Development of the Ego: Implications for Personality Theory, Psychopathology, and the Psychotherapeutic Process: By Stanley I. Greenspan. Madison, Connecticut: International Universities Press. 1989. Pp. 380. Int. J. Psycho-Anal., 73:179-181.

3. *What About Socialization?*
http://ochomeschooling.com/specialneeds/Socialization%20Myths.htm.homeschoolhelp@hotmail.com,

4. Ibid, *What About Socialization?*

5. Johnson, Robert, A., *Owning Your Own Shadow*, Harper Collins, 10 East 53rd St., New York, NY, 10022, 1993, Pg. 5.

6. *The Holy Bible*, King James Version, Job Chapter 42.

7, Gilmore, John, Dr. *A Return to Being Human Religiously*,

Iuniverse, Inc., Lincoln Nebraska, 68152, 2003, Page 1, Chapter 1.

8. Ibid., Pg 43, 44...

9. Ronin, Kendall, On Being Love's Warrior, Iuniverse Inc., Lincoln Nebraska 68512, www.dswellness.com, 2002, Pg. 2.

www.ingramcontent.com/pod-product-compliance
Lightning Source LLC
Chambersburg PA
CBHW022153080426
42734CB00006B/414